Understanding Trauma

Dr Roger Baker

Understanding Trauma

How to Overcome Post Traumatic Stress

LION

A Lion Book
an imprint of
Lion Hudson plc
Wilkinson House, Jordan Hill Road,
Oxford OX2 8DR, England
www.lionhudson.com

ISBN 978 0 7459 5379 3

Distributed by:
UK: Marston Book Services, PO Box 269, Abingdon, Oxon, OX14 4YN
USA: Trafalgar Square Publishing, 814 N. Franklin Street, Chicago, IL 60610
USA Christian Market: Kregel Publications, PO Box 2607, Grand Rapids, MI
49501

First edition 2010
10 9 8 7 6 5 4 3 2 1 0
All rights reserved

Acknowledgments
Page 93: Scripture quotation is from the *New International Version* published
by The Bible Societies/HarperCollins Publishers copyright © 1991, 1992,
1995 American Bible Society.

A catalogue record for this book is available from the British Library
Typeset in 9/12 ITC Stone Serif

Printed and bound in Great Britain by
Marston Book Services Ltd, Oxfordshire

Contents

Acknowledgments

I would like to acknowledge and thank all the patients who have generously allowed me to quote their cases. Most expressed the sentiment that "if it will help someone else, please use my case". Specific details about sessions are provided exactly as they happened, often with verbatim quotes from patients. There have been some minor changes to ensure cases are anonymous, such as age, occupation, towns, etc. In three cases there were major changes or elaborations: Jason (Chapter 1), Mr Wainwright (Chapter 3), and Claire (Chapter 4).

I would also like to thank Susan, who was not a patient but a friend, for sharing her story about the effect of an explosion and fire on a Hercules aircraft in which she was flying.

Especial thanks to Ann, my wife, who miraculously deciphered my handwritten chapters and typed them up, tidying up grammar and letting me know when I got too pompous or academic. Also thanks to Cathy Le Roux, my daughter, who read the near final chapters and gave me useful feedback.

Post Traumatic Stress Disorder

Chapter 1

A Life Spoiled

Jason was the smartest boy in class. He seemed to come top in every subject, and without much effort too. His teachers had marked him out for a place at Oxford or Cambridge University. And today was the last day at school – exams finished, career talks completed, end of term special social events over, and now, well, everyone was waiting for the bell that was to mark the start of the summer holiday. Jason looked at Mark, his closest friend, and grinned. The bell sounded and the whole class were off, quicker than a 100-metre start – running up the corridor, pelting down the stairs, rushing across the lawn, and then slowing to a leisurely walk through the school gates and to the pavement outside.

"I thought today would never end," said Jason.

"Too right," retorted Mark.

The two of them were rarely apart. In school they always sat together, outside school they were inseparable, and it was difficult to discern who lived in which home – that is what Jason's mother said, anyway. Mark's uncle nicknamed them the "terrible twins", although actually they weren't terrible at all, but quite well behaved for sixteen-year-old boys. Side by side they crossed the road and began walking down the pavement towards Mark's house, which was the nearest to the school. As Mark casually strolled on the outside of the pavement with Jason on the inside, they talked excitedly about the 101 things they would do now the holidays had really begun. As they chattered and laughed, a van pulled out of a side road from a house next to the school where they had been felling trees. The van was pulling a large trailer filled with sawn-off tree trunks and branches. There was something amiss. The overladen trailer was not balanced correctly and was badly out of sync with the movement of the van, swinging wildly from side to side. As the van turned into the main road, the trailer swung out and one of the tree trunks struck the two boys from behind as they walked along the pavement. It hit Mark on the hips and caught Jason's arm, breaking it instantly. Mark was caught up in the branches and dragged along by the van.

"The pain was excruciating," said Jason as he tearfully recounted the experience to me later. Jason had been referred to me by Kitson Jones Solicitors to assess the psychological impact of the accident that had occurred one year previously and to begin a course of psychological therapy to help him overcome his distress. Jason had made an excellent recovery from the broken arm, but the psychological damage of the accident seemed to have been much harder to heal.

"What exactly happened when the tree hit you?" I asked.

"It all seemed to happen in slow motion. There was the pain in my arm, and then I saw the van going past with Mark being thrown along behind it like a manikin – rolling, tumbling, tattered. It was a terrible sight. He was left lying still on the ground. I was sure he was dead." Jason paused and gazed at a point somewhere behind me. There was a long pause.

After a while, I asked "What happened next?"

"What happened next?" I repeated.

"He was left lying in the road. It was the worst sight I have ever seen, but someone said, 'Don't touch him.' I was in terrible pain from my broken arm and I couldn't believe this could happen to me. The van driver and his mate stopped and stared. I looked towards the tree trunk sticking out from the trailer and said, 'It's sticking out a mile.' I was so angry I wanted to hit them, but couldn't move my arm. Then they drove off, just drove off."

Jason was clearly distressed. He had had to recall the events for the solicitor a couple of times, but that had been an awkward, staccato affair, like a question and answer session. This was the first time he had recalled it in this amount of detail.

Jason's memory of what happened next was a bit hazy. An ambulance came and took Mark away first, then another came for him. He thinks he passed out on the way to hospital, and he remembered lying in a hospital bed. His memory of the time in hospital was nothing like as detailed as the accident itself, but he did recall he was there for about a week, though the time seemed to pass very slowly.

Shockwaves

Although Jason's physical recovery was remarkably quick and his arm was back to full strength in record time, his parents, his teachers, and he himself described himself as a "changed boy". Initially he did not want to leave the house. He felt a real sense of shock to realize that the world was no longer a safe place – that even pavements were dangerous places. He could barely trust anywhere again. On the day he eventually ventured out he had overwhelming flashbacks of Mark "like a rag doll", being pulled along the road behind the van. "They were so bad it brought me to tears," Jason confided.

He withdrew from meeting with his friends, and only wanted to see Mark (who had also recovered) on "good days". He refused to go on holiday with his parents or even attend the weekly lunch with his Gran. He seemed to have lost all his "oomph" to do things. His mother told me later that most of the time he spent just sitting and staring into space. He couldn't even bother to play games on his PC any more, whereas usually he couldn't be prised away from it.

When the summer holidays were over and school resumed, Jason's teachers soon noticed the change too – he seemed quiet and withdrawn, kept failing to give in his homework, made excuses, but, worst of all, did not seem to understand the lessons very well, which was most unusual. Jason said his memory seemed to be "mushy", and that all the time he felt like "a cat on hot bricks", too alert and too aroused to concentrate properly on what the teacher said. He would even jump out of his skin when there was a sudden noise in class or when a phone went off, and he had permanently switched off his mobile phone – his "life blood" – to avoid being startled. Sleep also was very difficult for him – it took him hours to drift off, and he would often awake in a sweat with a nightmare about being hit from behind, breaking his arm or leg, or being pulled along the ground.

His mother was very concerned about his "personality change". She said, "From being such a positive boy with loads of plans for the future, he has now got this funny idea about death. He told me he had cheated death this time, but that sooner or later it would come and get him. I think he's just waiting for death to come and get him." She felt that he had changed into "such a gloomy boy", and that whereas previously she could "chivvy" him out of a bad mood pretty easily, she just could not get him to look at the bright side of things any more.

What is This Strange Brew?

Jason had made a perfect physical recovery. He could use his arm without any pain or difficulty, and his friend Mark had made a good recovery too. He had not hit his head or suffered any neurological damage at all, yet he couldn't concentrate on his schoolwork, found it difficult to memorize what had previously been a "doddle", and longed for each day to finish so he could retreat to the silence of his room. Something had gone badly wrong. His parents knew it, his teachers knew it, and he knew it too. But what exactly had changed?

Was he suffering from some mental illness, some sort of psychosis in which his mental faculties were somehow diminished or damaged? Had his brain been permanently affected so that he no longer has the intellectual promise that was so obvious before? Could this be a mental breakdown?

When faced with the perplexity of such a changed life these are the sort of questions that the sufferer, and those around them, entertain. But this is neither psychosis nor brain damage, nor a mental breakdown. They don't come anywhere near to capturing what really had happened.

Jason was experiencing what has come to be known as "Post Traumatic Stress Disorder" (PTSD). The unusual and powerful symptoms of PTSD often lead sufferers to conclude that they have "lost it", "had a breakdown", "gone mad", or that some catastrophic process has changed their life forever.

Most people have experienced stress in one form or another – we all know about the dentist, the anxious wait for an exam, competing in a race, having to give a talk in front of an audience, the job interview. All these seem to be able to reduce us to jelly, yet these experiences are nothing like what Jason was going through. His experiences seemed to be in a realm of their own – things he had never before experienced in his life. It was this unusual quality about the stress symptoms that naturally led him to the thought of madness or "losing it".

Post Traumatic Stress Disorder

Post Traumatic Stress Disorder, as the words suggest, is a particular stress reaction following a trauma. In Jason's case the trauma was being hit from behind by a tree trunk. The trauma engenders the reaction, and not everyone develops this disorder after a trauma. Many people, after suffering some degree of psychological shock after a trauma, go on to adjust well, with it having little effect on their lives. Others can be debilitated from the same event. Not only does this depend on the person, but also on the nature of the trauma. Here is a list of some of the traumas that can set off Post Traumatic Stress Disorder:

- car or motorbike crashes; being hit by a car
- railway accidents; accidents at sea or in the air
- accidents at work or in the home
- electrocution, drowning, falls
- fires
- natural disasters, such as hurricanes, floods, forest fires, earthquakes
- loss of a limb; breast or organ removal
- being burned, wounded, or having emergency surgery
- diagnosis of life-threatening disease; frightening medical interventions; the return of a cancerous growth
- heart attacks
- trauma during childbirth
- robberies, bank hold-ups, muggings, thefts, assault, stabbing, being attacked with a weapon
- attack by an animal
- being wounded
- wounding or killing others
- physical or sexual abuse as a child
- physical or sexual abuse in the marital relationship
- rape
- torture
- life as a refugee, in a prison or concentration camp
- being caught up in oppressive and controlling religious cult
- wartime combat
- being caught in a war zone as a civilian, journalist, or refugee
- gun shots, explosions, bombings
- being a hostage
- witnessing horrific injury or deaths
- hearing about violence or murder of those you love
- near-death experience.

Some traumas are more noxious than others. Accidents, natural disasters, and witnessing others being harmed are traumatic but produce fewer psychological casualties than wartime combat and physical assault. The trauma that produces the highest risk for developing Post Traumatic Stress Disorder is rape; 65 per cent of men and 46 per cent of women develop PTSD after rape.[1] It is also hard to escape the effects of repeated or prolonged trauma, such as with concentration camp survivors. At one time PTSD was referred to as "a normal reaction to an abnormal event". The idea behind this was that the Post Traumatic reaction was normal enough, not mad or aberrant, but the trauma itself was the culprit. What has changed in this often-used phrase is not the first part, "a normal reaction", but the second, "to an abnormal event". No longer can trauma be regarded as an abnormal event. In a nationwide survey of 5,800 adult residents in the US who were interviewed in their homes, 61 per cent of men and 51 per cent of women reported experiencing at least one traumatic event in their lifetime. The most common events were witnessing someone being injured or killed (25 per cent), being involved in a fire or natural disaster (17 per cent) and being involved in a life-threatening accident (20 per cent).[2] In another study, a telephone survey of 2,200 adults in the Detroit area, 60 per cent of those interviewed had experienced the sudden, unexpected death of a loved one in their lifetime.[3]

So what we have is "a normal reaction to a not so abnormal event".

This book is all about that reaction – exactly what constitutes a Post Traumatic Stress reaction, the devastating effect it has on the person's life and those close to them, how it can it be treated, and, the $64,000 question, how it can be prevented.

Why Did I Write This Book?

In 1995 I wrote the self-help book *Understanding Panic Attacks and Overcoming Fear.*[4] At that time I was working in a psychology department that was in the forefront of research on panic attacks, and I was personally seeing many panic sufferers for psychological therapy and in research interviews. I updated the book in 2003 to include new understandings from emotion research. I don't know how it happened, but in the last ten years my clinical work has changed to almost exclusively treating Post Traumatic Stress sufferers. Over the years so many patients have told me how much *Understanding Panic Attacks* has helped them that I thought, "Why not do the same for Post Traumatic Stress Disorder?" So *Understanding Trauma* was born.

The purposes of writing this book are:

1. To provide information about Post Traumatic Stress Disorder for the reader who just wishes to know more about the topic.

2. This book is written especially for those caught in the grip of a bewildering Post Traumatic Stress experience, as well as those who have largely overcome trauma but may still be experiencing a few persistent and annoying symptoms. It is possible that the reader may know that something is wrong but not be sure how to categorize it or make sense of the experience. Hopefully this book will help them to pinpoint whether they are or are not suffering from Post Traumatic Stress Disorder and what they can do about it.

3. To prepare PTSD sufferers for psychological therapy; to help them to understand what might be involved; and possibly to guide them in deciding whether to seek the help of a psychological therapist.

4. Some people prefer not to go to a therapist, but would rather "do it themselves". So this book describes in detail for the first time a self-help emotional processing programme for those suffering from Post Traumatic Stress Disorder.

5. To help relatives and friends of those suffering from the condition to understand what is happening.

6. To help others understand the importance of emotional processing and how it works, providing a useful life skill that allows them to maximize their own healing potential. An improved emotional processing style should not only reduce vulnerability for developing PTSD and other conditions such as panic disorder, but also act as the first preparatory stage for the successful treatment of PTSD.

Outline of the Book

To give readers a full understanding of PTSD, the book has been divided into five main sections.

Section I is designed to come to grips with exactly what PTSD is, giving the reader a good understanding of the disorder. Chapter 2 describes every symptom of PTSD, with illustrations from patients and sufferers in order to give a really clear picture of what are sometimes inexplicable feelings. Chapter 3, "Post Traumatic Stress in the Dock", clarifies what sort of psychological mechanisms underlie these symptoms, providing an understanding of why the unusual symptoms develop. Chapter 4 is an autobiographical account of Claire, injured in a domestic accident. It tries to address the often-asked question "Why me?" The first section of the book, then, is full of examples and case histories, so the reader can become familiar with what at first is a perplexing picture of "weird" reactions.

Section II moves from the arena of individual patients' symptoms to provide a greater psychological understanding of PTSD. Chapter 5 introduces "Emotional Processing", the way in which people deal with and get over psychological stress. If we learn to move with this natural system instead of fighting against it we have the basic building blocks for overcoming even the most severe trauma. Chapter 6, "Burying the Memories", examines how the memories of a traumatic event are stored, describing "hot memories" imbued with excessive emotional power. This provides the background for understanding how flashbacks and nightmares suddenly intrude in consciousness. It describes two ways of controlling memories: suppression, which is a voluntary act of will, and dissociation, in which the mind involuntarily cuts off the memory. Both of these mechanisms hinder the natural emotional processing of the traumatic memory and, as it were, lock the memory away. Chapter 7, "Emotions, the Stuff of Life", goes into emotions in more depth, showing how they are vital to a happy, healthy life, and explains in detail how emotions can be distorted in Post Traumatic Stress. These chapters are quite psychological in their approach, as opposed to the rather practical and concrete examples from patients' lives in Section I. It is important though to understand the psychological underpinnings of emotional processing, to pave the way to how PTSD can be overcome.

Section III explores healthy reactions to trauma and identifies the point at which psychological therapy becomes necessary. Chapter 8 describes Susan, a diplomat posted in Afghanistan, caught in a horrific air crash. It is a wonderful reminder of a healthy reaction to a trauma, of how even extreme adversity can be overcome. I asked Susan to write this chapter to act as a sort of counterpoint in the book, to remind both the reader and me that Post Traumatic Stress Disorder does not have to occur, and that it is the exception rather than the rule. Chapter 9 explores further what constitutes a healthy reaction to trauma and how to apply this in the first few weeks after a trauma. It also tackles the knotty question of whether Post Traumatic Stress Disorder can be prevented by developing the right emotional processing style for handling distress. Chapter 10 introduces Emotional Processing Therapy and explores exactly how emotional processing operates in overcoming PTSD, providing the background theory for the self-help programme to follow in Section IV.

Section IV is more of a "how to" guide. It explains what happens in Emotional Processing Therapy and covers in detail how it is possible to conduct self-therapy. The general recommendation is to seek out a good therapist, and the section gives recommendations for what to look for. Some people, however, prefer to overcome PTSD themselves, and so it covers in detail what to do. It starts off in Chapter 11 by describing the course of therapy for Max, who developed PTSD after falling from a roof in his work as a window cleaner. Max made a good recovery, and the details of his therapy help to provide the flavour of what Emotional Processing Therapy is all about. It encourages an open and accepting approach to emotions rather than avoiding and suppressing emotional experience. Chapter 12 is about preparing for therapy: what are the different options for therapy; how suitable self-help might be; what is treatable and what is not. Chapter 13, "Emotional Processing Style", explores what a healthy approach to emotions might be and presents a new self-rating scale to help people assess the strengths and weaknesses of their own emotional processing style. Chapter 14 explains why facing the memories of the trauma is so important, but can be very demanding, so time is devoted to explaining how to make the right sort of preparations to start this part of therapy. It then describes how to face the difficult memories, how to continue until PTSD symptoms become minimal, and, importantly, how to deal with setbacks.

Section V explores specific issues and complications in PTSD and common stumbling blocks to successful therapy. It revolves around the case of Jules, who had a ruptured appendix, which cascaded into other traumas in his long and difficult period of recovery in hospital. This chapter shows just how complicated a trauma can get and explores some of the factors that may effect recovery from PTSD.

The concluding chapter discusses a relatively new finding that has emerged from the study and treatment of Post Traumatic Stress Disorder – that although distressing PTSD symptoms can seriously impair people's lives, the opposite, "Post Traumatic Growth", is often found too. It seems that a paradox exists that out of the depths of distressing and disabling symptoms, personal growth and empowerment can also be found.

The book finally returns to the theme of emotional processing as a sort of second immune system, not dealing with physical viruses and bacteria, but rather with emotional hurts and traumas. When we learn to work with and respect this valuable natural process, then recovery and therapy comes into sight. Emotional processing holds the key not just to overcoming Post Traumatic Stress Disorder, but also to a more fulfilling emotional experience and possibly to preventing PTSD in the first place.

Although the book was written to help those with PTSD, readers don't have to personally be suffering from PTSD to get something out of it – sometimes just the detailed knowledge of a disorder can be of great value in its own right. In view of the finding that trauma is not such an abnormal event after all, knowing how to face trauma and minimize its worst ravages is a skill we can all benefit from.

Chapter 2

What is Post Traumatic Stress Disorder?

While most emotional or psychological problems are difficult to pin down, this is not the case with Post Traumatic Stress Disorder. At one time, "Shell Shock", "Battle Fatigue", or "Fright Neuroses" were different terms that army doctors used to try to capture the essence of what they were seeing with traumatized soldiers. But in 1980, the American Psychiatric Association, which publishes diagnostic manuals for the guidance of psychiatrists and psychologists, first introduced the diagnosis of "Post Traumatic Stress Disorder". In the years preceding 1980, expert committees had gathered many clinical observations and research studies on trauma that pointed to a single disorder, which they named "Post Traumatic Stress Disorder". What was new was that it was not just confined to battle trauma but applied to any of the multiple traumas that can befall human beings. Not only did the American Psychiatric Association describe the new disorder in the *Diagnostic and Statistical Manual of Mental Disorders III* but they gave clear criteria for what constitutes PTSD and how to diagnose it. This has become accepted throughout the world and generated a huge amount of research into PTSD. What I want to do in this chapter is to explain what constitutes PTSD, describing what the symptoms and experiences are that make it up, according to the *Diagnostic and Statistical Manual* "the fourth version" (*DSM-IV*) of the American Psychiatric Association.[1] Someone referring to the Ten Commandments once said, "Well, they're not exactly set in stone, are they?" Post Traumatic Stress Disorder has been set in stone by the *Diagnostic and Statistical Manual*, which makes my task rather easy.

I will use the exact wording of *DSM-IV* to describe the symptoms of PTSD followed by a real-life example of the experience.

Diagnostic Criteria for Post Traumatic Stress Disorder

A. The person has been exposed to a traumatic event in which both of the following were present:

1. The person experienced, witnessed, or was confronted with an event or events that involved actual or threatened death or serious injury, or a threat to the physical integrity of self or others.

2. The person's response involved intense fear, helplessness, or horror.

The traumatic event may take many shapes and forms but it involves personally experiencing a situation that might cause your death or injury, or witnessing others being injured or dying. Watching someone die in a movie does not have this impact because it is not personal and immediate. In trauma the reality hits you. The feelings of fear, helplessness, or horror are indicators that you have emotionally registered the reality.

A German woman described the first big air raid on a German city during World War II as follows:

I saw people killed by falling bricks and heard the screams of others dying in the fire. I dragged my best friend from a burning building and she died in my arms. I saw others who went stark mad. The shock to my nerves and to the soul, one can never erase.[2]

B. The traumatic event is persistently re-experienced in one (or more) of the following ways:

1. Recurrent and intrusive distressing recollections of the event, including images, thoughts, or perceptions.

2. Recurrent distressing dream of the event.

3. Acting or feeling as if the traumatic event were recurring (includes a sense of reliving the experience, illusions, hallucinations, and dissociative flashback episodes, including those that occur on awakening or when intoxicated).

4. Intense psychological distress at exposure to internal or external cues that symbolize or resemble an aspect of the traumatic event.

5. Physiological reactivity on exposure to internal or external cues that symbolize or resemble an aspect of the traumatic event.

1. Recurrent and intrusive distressing recollections of the event, including images, thoughts, or perceptions.

These are often referred to as flashbacks. Mrs S. had witnessed the car in front of her hit a cyclist. She got out of her car and ran to the cyclist to try to help. It was the sight of him lying still on the road that lately kept flashing into her mind, like a snapshot. As she told me about this in the interview she said, "As I am talking to you I can see him on the floor." Another man described flashbacks as like "little snippets of what happened". While it is normal for people to think about the event over and over of their own volition in an attempt to understand and put all the pieces together, flashbacks are against the person's will, and force themselves like intruders into their consciousness. One woman said she wished they would "leave me alone", as if the memories almost had a separate identity. They are often accompanied by the same feeling the person experienced during the trauma, or sickening feelings of fear, and are very vivid.

Some people have the sense of reliving the trauma in the present during a flashback, while others experience them as powerful memories of the past. The flashbacks can be visual – "I suddenly see the face of the intruder"; they can be sounds – one motorcyclist said, "The sound of the impact will never leave me." Some people describe feelings – "During the day I feel jolted just like I was in the crash; it's rather like the feeling of falling when you're just getting off to sleep", or smells – "I keep smelling my own blood; it makes me nauseous all day." They usually last a few minutes but can be short (seconds), or even last hours.

Flashbacks can be the most distressing feature of PTSD. I asked one client to explain to me what having a flashback felt like. He said, "My heart palpitates; it takes my breath away, I think I'm going to panic. Momentarily my vision goes, not a complete blackout, but away from the world around me." One man couldn't eat or sleep after a flashback, and often phoned his mother for help. Another felt "shaky and tired" and "sat quietly for ages" with his mind a blank. For some, particularly soon after the trauma, the distressing recollections may be there "all the time" or "in the background all the time like a weird feeling of tempting fate", and they may find, "I can't get rid of them." What makes flashbacks frightening is that they are so powerful that they are out of the realms of normal experience; as one man put it, "so tangible, I could touch it".

2. Recurrent distressing dream of the event.

Sometimes nightmares are direct replays of the trauma, sometimes variations around the theme of the trauma. Natalie was diagnosed with breast cancer and received chemotherapy and radiotherapy without showing any significant signs of trauma. However it was two weeks after her breast operation that her persistent nightmares started; after the operation, when the bandages had been removed, she had stood in front of the mirror looking at her scar. She was horrified to have "no breast left", that it was final and definitive – "it can never come back again". Shortly afterwards the nightmares (and other PTSD symptoms) started. In her dream the cancer had returned and she was on the operating table having both breasts removed, with voices anxiously saying that "we can't get it all out" as the surgeons cut deeper and deeper into her chest to try to remove all the cancer. Meanwhile her children stood round the operating table crying. Natalie would awake crying, sweating, and with her heart pounding. The same dream recurred four to six times per week.

The human mind groups disasters around themes relevant to oneself, whether it be danger, personal loss, mutilation, guilt, or death. It depends on the most significant elements for that individual and how they typically symbolize events. For Natalie her preoccupation revolved around breast surgery, not being able to get rid of cancer, and sorrow for the whole family.

When John F. described how a faulty industrial saw at work severed his fingers, somehow the sound of the saw was an important part of the horrific experience. His mind had fixed on the significance of noise, which permeated his "anxiety dreams" in the form of "ear piercing noises, increasing in frequency, of aircraft flying low, and explosives". The mind is capable of symbolizing events in many ways and for John it was in terms of loud noises of many types. Whatever the content of the dream, the person often awakes sweating, breathless, with palpitations, and full of fear.

Sometimes nightmares can occur several times a night, so that the person may wish to actually avoid sleep. In the attempt to avoid nightmares and generally improve their appalling sleep, many will drink alcohol to excess or take sleeping tablets. One patient told me that he took seven sleeping tablets instead of the prescribed one, or he could drink two bottles of wine, and he would still wake up with nightmares. The nightmares, which were the most frightening feature of PTSD for him, made him despair so much he was prepared to do almost anything to stop them. The nightmares are often obvious to the partner too; they might describe the person as "thrashing about" in bed, crying in their sleep, shouting out, or jumping out of bed.

3. Acting or feeling as if the traumatic event were recurring (includes a sense of reliving the experience, illusions, hallucinations, and dissociative flashback episodes, including those that occur on awakening or when intoxicated).

Although this is less common than flashbacks or nightmares, the person can have the feeling that they are "in" the trauma, re-experiencing it all over again. In a study of 525 World War II prisoners of war from Alsace-Lorraine, who survived captivity in the USSR,[3] it was found that nearly all the survivors experienced a range of severe PTSD symptoms. Eighty-four per cent reported recurrent distressing dreams or nightmares of wartime and captivity events still present when the study was conducted forty-five years after their captivity. This is the author's summary of "acting or feeling as if the traumatic event were recurring":

> *While we examined them, the men often described reliving, or "seeing again", their experiences in camp. At these times, they became noticeably ill at ease and distracted. They appeared conspicuously detached from their surroundings and were anxious and appeared to be dissociating. Moist hands and other symptoms of somatic anxiety were often observed during the interviews. The re-experiencing of captivity was also provoked by a variety of other recent events... some events were easily associated with experiences of captivity (an orchestra playing Russian music). Another man described the sudden feeling of being back in a Kolkhoz (collective farm) when he entered a crowded city square.*

4. Intense psychological distress at exposure to internal or external cues that symbolize or resemble an aspect of the traumatic event.

Mr M., a mechanic who maintained coaches for a coach company, had been trapped under a coach that had collapsed when he was doing repairs underneath it, and to make things worse the driver drove the wheels over him in an attempt to set him free. He only had to see the word "Abbey" (the name of the firm) to bring intense psychological distress. The smell of tyres, seeing a coach pass him in the street, enclosed dark spaces, especially if he was lying down in a way similar to when he was trapped under the coach, made him nervous and angry. Talking about the accident, which is an "external cue" symbolizing the accident, or even thinking about it, an "internal cue", could powerfully bring back distressing memories.

At times the cues can be very broad and impinge into large areas of the person's life. One rape victim during therapy[4] said:

I have a very difficult time trusting men, especially when left alone with them. I'm scared, always thinking in the back of my mind how I would defend myself if that man were to attack me. It bothers me that I feel that way and do not trust many people. Before the rape, when I was left alone with a man, my thoughts always drifted to... was he interested in me, did he find me attractive. After the rape, I would get the shakes being left alone with a man.

Here the "external cue" that symbolizes the traumatic event is men. The problem with rape is actually much greater than this because other than just "men" the number of possible cues that trigger distress can be enormous – darkness, being alone, noisy people, being in bed – so that hardly anything is safe any more.

At other times the cues can be very specific: one man could drive on most roads, including motorways, at nearly all times, but had great difficulty if driving along country lanes at dusk.

5. Physiological reactivity on exposure to internal or external cues that symbolize or resemble an aspect of the traumatic event.

This refers to bodily sensations that may be triggered off, as distinct from "psychological distress". In practice both psychological distress and "physiological reactivity" often go together.

Silvia was a 53-year-old woman who had been treated for breast cancer three years earlier, and although making a good physical recovery she was experiencing Post Traumatic Stress reactions. For her, the greatest trauma was her experience of chemotherapy – after the discovery and diagnosis of a malignant mass in her left breast she was assigned (with her permission) to a drug trial using a new preparation for chemotherapy. The "chemo" went badly wrong – she had an extreme reaction to the chemical infusion and had to be removed from the trial. As she described the chemo to me three years later, in tears, she reported that a particular colour of red, the same colour as the chemo infusion, still makes her feel nauseous. Not any red colour; she was carrying her notes in a pillar-box red folder which caused no distress, and she wore a pink chiffon scarf:

> *It's just a certain red… even to think about that sort of red makes me feel… it brings back all the sick feeling and makes me feel a bit shaky. When I came into the ward today I had to sit quietly downstairs before I came up. When I'm up and see all the people [tears at this point] I feel so sorry and thankful for the help I got. It's a weak-ish red. I had a cranberry juice two days ago, and it suddenly flicked everything back and I told myself not to be so silly and drink it.*

C. Persistent avoidance of stimuli associated with the trauma and numbing of general responsiveness as indicated by three or more of the following:

Note that there are two categories of symptoms here – avoidance (symptoms 1 and 2) and numbing (symptoms 3–7).

1. *Efforts to avoid thoughts, feelings, or conversations associated with the trauma.*
2. *Efforts to avoid activities, places, or people that arouse recollections of the trauma.*
3. *Inability to recall an important aspect of the trauma.*
4. *Markedly diminished interest in participation in significant activities.*
5. *Feeling of detachment or estrangement from others.*
6. *Restricted range of affect (e.g. unable to have loving feelings).*
7. *Sense of foreshortened future (e.g. does not expect to have a career, marriage, children, or a normal lifespan).*

1. Efforts to avoid thoughts, feelings or conversations associated with the trauma.

Here are some of the types of avoidance reported by the patients:

- "Avoiding looking at similar situations on TV."
- "I prefer to avoid discussing that day."
- "I try to avoid the [memory of] the car coming towards me."

- "Not spending much time on my own" (in order not to think about the trauma).
- "I try to stop thinking about it, but the second of the impact pops into my mind."
- "Thoughts of the landslide come to mind but I try to block them out by thinking of something else."
- "I used to panic if I picked up the phone and it was something connected to the violence. I told whoever it was to call back later."
- "Every time the thought comes I try to avoid it by shaking it out of my head."

Mrs R. described it as "always in the back of my mind. I try hard to control how much I consciously think of the accident."

Peter summarized what many patients feel when he said:

I try my hardest not to think about the crash but the more I try to push away the thoughts the more they would intrude, which was really annoying. All in all, the attempt to avoid memories of the trauma is pretty exhausting.

2. Efforts to avoid activities, places, or people that arouse recollections of the trauma.

Again this is related to avoidance, but the more concrete avoidance of people and places rather than thoughts or feelings.

After a bike accident, Mr T. avoided going out of his house. He said, "It is impossible to go anywhere without the noise of cars accelerating and braking. I can't get away from it. Now I just lock myself away. It's too big for me – too much danger."

Other things people may avoid include:
- walking past the scene of an accident
- travel by train or plane
- driving/being a passenger/driving at night or on motorways
- going to hospital (where an operation went wrong)
- watching things on TV that remind them of hospitals, such as *ER* or *Animal Hospital*
- looking at a part of their body which has been damaged in an accident

Zena, who was attacked by an intruder in her house at night, could not sleep in the same bed and preferred to sleep downstairs in an armchair with the light on. Beatrice, who was attacked in a shop, avoided small shops like the one in which she was attacked and men who resembled the man who attacked her.

It is sometimes nearly impossible to avoid some things. Jane T. said, "I try to avoid driving but I have to drive to work. If I could get there by telepathic travel I'd quite happily do it."

3. Inability to recall an important aspect of the trauma.

This applies more to a psychological blockage in recall rather than any physical effect of a trauma, such as being knocked unconscious or being given morphine.

Mrs G. said, "I would say there were definite blanks in my memory of the accident. It seems different from normal forgetfulness – it's almost as if you can pick bits out that have been extracted. You can't see these bits in between."

Mrs I. said, "The scene of the disaster is hazy. I just felt shock and unbelief and seemed to go into a rather numb and detached state for a few days."

4. Markedly diminished interest in participation in significant activities.

This often involves reduced interest in socializing, going out, talking, hobbies previously enjoyed, watching TV, reading, eating, and sexual relations.

Tara said, "I have lost interest in socializing and in material things. I don't go shopping as much and would rather stay at home where I feel safer. I used to read a book a day, but don't read as much now. I made myself go skiing to prove I could still do it."

James still socialized but noticed that "before I would take the lead in what we did or where we went, but now I go along with others or wait for them to decide first".

5. Feeling of detachment or estrangement from others.

6. Restricted range of affect (e.g. unable to have loving feelings).

I would like to deal with these next two symptoms together, because experimental studies have shown they are closely related, and it is often thought that the estrangement from others is due to not being able to feel emotions properly. These two symptoms are often referred to as "emotional anaesthesia" or "psychological numbing".

"Emotional anaesthesia" and the consequent difficulties in having close relationships is a feature of severe, prolonged trauma, such as that experienced by holocaust victims and those caught up in horrific warfare. In order to survive the impossible horror of warfare or concentration camps the mind can automatically "close off". One trauma researcher explained it like this: "All feelings ceased to be, at least on the surface, because one could not exist and at the same time live with such feelings of abhorrence, disgust and terror."[5] Soldiers who experience appalling atrocities are often described as "cold, unfeeling, and uncaring" by their partners when they return home, and relationship problems and marriage breakdown is common. It has been suggested that memories of the trauma are so dreadful that inner peace is only gained by maintaining a "dead space" or retreating into "mental foxholes".[6]

While emotional anaesthesia may be more common after the repeated and appalling atrocities of war, it is less common in "one-off" traumas such as a car crash. Often when I ask clients whether they are unable to experience loving feelings, they cannot identify with this but on the contrary say they feel closer to their loved ones.

7. Sense of foreshortened future (e.g. does not expect to have a career, marriage, children, or a normal lifespan).

The following discussion on a PTSD Internet forum[7] provides an illustration of this symptom.

Esther: "I just realized that the belief I had of dying in the near future was a symptom of PTSD. I don't fully understand why trauma would cause this, can anybody shed some light?"

Really down: "Hi, Esther, welcome to the forum. I thought that I would die early ever since the age of seven or so but I always thought it was normal... i.e. that everyone thought about it. Not until a few years ago in college, when we covered a story in which a character imagines his/her own funeral and the prof's subsequent discussion of how unusual this is, did it occur to me that it could be because of the trauma. Actually, at that time, while I had the memories, I had no idea that I had PTSD. I think that because trauma causes us to feel scared for our lives and those of others... we just keep waiting for something to happen... It's hard for me to articulate this.

Sometimes, perhaps, we also feel that we don't deserve to live that long. Or the trauma shatters our illusions and therefore we can't imagine living a long, full life…"

D. Persistent symptoms of increased arousal (not present before the trauma) as indicated by two or more of the following:

1. Difficulty falling or staying asleep

2. Irritability or outbursts of anger

3. Difficulty concentrating

4. Hypervigilance

5. Exaggerated startle response

This group of symptoms all represent a state of increased arousal or anxiety engendered by the trauma. Some of these symptoms, such as problems with sleep and concentration, are not specific to PTSD but can occur when someone is generally under stress, or is experiencing significant anxiety or depression. Hypervigilance (being constantly on the look-out for danger) and exaggerated startle response are a bit more specific to PTSD. One important feature of high arousal not mentioned in *DSM-IV* is the occurrence of panic attacks, which represent a level where high arousal trips over, as it were, into a full-blown panic attack.

1. Difficulty falling or staying asleep

Difficulty falling or staying asleep may be a result of the person's generally high level of arousal, so that their "starting point" is so high it is difficult to relax and drift into a deep sleep. Alternatively, as nightmares and bad dreams are so common in PTSD, they may jolt the person as they are trying to go to sleep, or wake them in a state of fear during the night. The fear of having a nightmare can also cast a shadow over sleep and can lead to heavy drinking, which can disrupt sleep patterns and contribute to early wakening. Poor sleep may play a part in other symptoms in this list such as irritability. Worry about poor sleep and how it can incapacitate performance can further aggravate the problem. Another cause of poor sleep in PTSD may be that during the trauma the person's injury or loss of a limb can cause them pain and wake them from sleep. Sometimes the pain itself is a reminder of the trauma and can set off flashbacks in the day or nightmares at night.

2. Irritability or outbursts of anger

This is one of those symptoms of PTSD that people often find confusing. Before, they may have been easygoing, enjoying a laugh and a joke, but now they find themselves shouting at their children, losing their temper over little things, being snappy and irritable. It's not surprising that they feel there's been some sort of character change. Elaine, after a house burglary in which she and her husband were punched and tied up, described becoming extremely intolerant, especially with her family, and had upset friends and family, and lost friends. She was more opinionated and outspoken and easily got angry with others. She felt her "fuse was much shorter. John [her husband] will make a joke and I jump down his throat." This was very much out of character, because she was normally bubbly and sociable. She really felt "I've changed as a person," but had put this down to age and tiredness and did not realize it was a typical symptom of PTSD. It simply does not represent a permanent "personality change" because as the person recovers from PTSD the irritability leaves them too.

3. Difficulty concentrating

This includes concentrating on and understanding what others say, concentrating on everyday activities, reading, watching TV, memorizing things, and generally "keeping on the job". What is central here is cognitive control – maintaining a focused attention on the task until it is achieved.

Lucy was able to successfully juggle doing a part-time degree with administrative work at a local insurance firm. She had been raped by a group of youths at a rock concert ten months earlier and suffered what she called "a breakdown". She had, however, made a reasonable recovery in getting back to her office work. She told me:

At work I have to concentrate. I work in an office with three others and I'm interrupted a lot. I'm used to this and am coping quite well. At home, when I'm watching a film, my concentration is rubbish. I'm easily distracted and haven't seen a film through. I'm reading a lot less, which I can't afford to do with my finals looming. I pick on simpler books or just read a chapter at a time. I should be doing two hours of typing on my dissertation but just go and do something else.

Jack used to read the paper avidly every day. Now he can't watch films, read books, or read the paper. "I try to read, but do not have patience. It's not sinking in."

Sometimes the problem is lack of understanding, such as not following a conversation or having to read the same sentence several times to understand it; sometimes it's not being able to memorize a sequence of events, such as not being able to retain the plot of a film; sometimes it's the lack of "oomph" to stay concentrating; and sometimes it's being easily distracted by other things or being absorbed by the memory of the trauma. Jack had told me his memory was poor "apart from my memory of the accident". Mr R. said, "I used to laugh and joke before, but my humour is cutting and sarcastic now. If I've got to do something I can't wait until it's done. I want to get it done and get back to my own little world." His "own little world" was thinking about his amputation over and over again.

4. Hypervigilance

Hypervigilance goes with danger. If you are a soldier on patrol, hypervigilance, that is being especially alert to danger, is very sensible. Spotting danger quickly may save your life. The trauma that is at the heart of Post Traumatic Stress Disorder is related to danger; the threat to one's life, whether it is an accident, injury, or battle situation, has broken through the barriers of normal everyday safety and had a profound impact. The emotional message etched into one's memory is "danger". The soldier after his foot patrol is over can afford to relax in barracks and cease his hypervigilant approach. Unfortunately in PTSD the emotion-based memory will not rest in the same way, but keeps transmitting the same "danger" message. The message won't switch off, so the person is constantly alert for new dangers even though the traumatic event is long past. In the previous chapter I described how Jason would not initially venture into the streets or walk down pavements because everything that had previously seemed safe and normal was now dangerous. He was expecting danger and was vigilant about every movement of cars or pedestrians around him. Sometimes the hypervigilance gets narrowed down to the focal event. Jason eventually was able to walk on pavements facing traffic and travel in cars but was never comfortable walking down pavements with his back to the traffic. For other traumas, however, the range of danger "stimuli" is just too large so that the person is over-vigilant on a near permanent basis. Resick and Schnicke in their book *Cognitive Processing Therapy for Rape Victims*[8] illustrate just how broad these "danger signals" can be for rape victims. They quote from a woman who was raped as an adolescent:

> *The person I was before no longer exists. It means that I no longer feel safe, even during daylight hours. I used to believe that rape happened to beautiful women sometime during the night, and somewhere secluded, a world away from me. I thought it was something that I would have to worry about only when I was an adult. My experience shattered every one of those beliefs, and now it's hard to determine what to believe – what is true and who can be trusted.*
>
> *Being raped means that I now will not allow myself to be relaxed enough to let loose, to let go. I have to be in control at all times, and will make every effort to separate myself from a situation where I don't feel that I have some control, some way of calling the shots. I am a control freak in my relationships. This makes intimacy difficult. Since I was raped, I do not trust men, any of them! For a while I was even afraid of my own father, a man who would never hurt anyone, let alone his own daughter. I constantly wonder if I am trusting the right people. I never saw who raped me – how can I know who is trustworthy?*

So many things we normally take for granted have become "dangerous" – daytime, crowded situations, being natural and spontaneous, intimacy, and men of all types.

5. Exaggerated startle response

This is another sign of over-arousal. Most of us can be startled by a really loud bang or someone jumping out on us from nowhere. In PTSD the response is exaggerated – even innocuous things can trigger a startle reaction, such as the phone or doorbell ringing. One client described herself as very "jumpy". This would occur if someone approached her from behind or the doorbell rang: "My jumpiness is something of a joke at work. I absolutely jump out of my skin."

E. Duration of the disturbance (re-experiencing, avoidance, numbing, and increased arousal) is more than one month.

While it is normal to have strong experiences such as a sense of numbing or detachment, flashbacks, nightmares, and over-arousal immediately after a traumatic event, a marked reaction persisting over a longer time period comes into the category of PTSD. One month is the time that *DSM-IV* has specified as the start of PTSD. One month is not a magical time when a normal reaction suddenly metamorphoses into Post Traumatic Stress Disorder; it's a rule of thumb to indicate that PTSD refers to a more long-lasting condition. Many of the patients seen for psychological therapy have had PTSD symptoms for longer than one month. The slow moving medico-legal process means that assessment, therapy, and compensation for accident victims can be delayed and many have suffered from PTSD symptoms for two to three years. Without treatment it is a potentially long-lasting condition. In the case of soldiers from Alsace-Lorraine who had been in Russian captivity (quoted earlier), the majority still experienced PTSD symptoms forty-five years later. This is also the case for holocaust survivors or those who had experienced atrocities over a prolonged period.

F. The disturbance causes clinically significant distress or impairment in social, occupational, or other important areas of functioning.

Many of the symptoms of PTSD are intrinsically distressing – nightmares, flashbacks, sleep problems, and irritability – but become even more troubling if the person does not understand what is happening. The description of the various symptoms in this chapter is an attempt to increase understanding and lessen misconceptions about this being mental illness. In a way, the greater the number and the severity of PTSD symptoms, the harder it would be not to show "clinically significant distress or impairment".

Other symptoms, such as diminished interest or participation in significant events, or avoiding places or people that arouse recollections of the trauma, imply social restriction. Feelings of detachment or estrangement from others or restricted range of affect suggest impairment in personal relationships, one aspect of which is loss of sexual intimacy. The intrusiveness of nightmares and flashbacks and symptoms of increased arousal such as irritability, difficulty concentrating, and hypervigilance can threaten work performance.

In this chapter I have quoted examples of patients who have returned to work despite their PTSD symptoms. As clinicians we could quote other examples of those unable to return to work, whose marriages have soured and collapsed, who have pulled out of former social activities and contacts and lost friends. For some, not only do they have nightmares, but also their whole life has *become* a nightmare.

Mrs E., quoted in Beverly Raphael's book *When Disaster Strikes*,[9] is a sad example of impairment that reaches its lowest ebb:

Mrs E., aged fifty, could not believe that her son Alan, the "light of her life", could have been killed in an air disaster. She did not see his body and felt it was all some terrible nightmare. She kept her son's room untouched and grew increasingly angry at her husband's attempts to reinvolve her in life. She would spend many hours in her son's room, which she kept as a "memorial to the most wonderful young man who ever lived". Enlarged photos of her son filled the house. In the evenings she would hold long conversations with him. Her whole family was in despair because she rejected all offers of help. Her picture of unresolved grief, with tears, anger and despair, continued unabated for four years.

Set in Stone?

I mentioned at the beginning of this chapter that PTSD had been "set in stone" in the American Psychiatric Association's *Diagnostic and Statistical Manual*. All the symptoms are clearly specified. But you may have noticed that within the main symptoms categories (B: Re-experiencing, C: Avoidance, and D: Increased Arousal) the diagnosis can be made if sufficient numbers of different symptoms are present from the "menu". For instance, avoidance and numbing are "as indicated by three (or more) of the following...". It has been calculated that there are 175 different permutations of symptoms that can be called Post Traumatic Stress Disorder. So it is not so much a single fixed illness with specific signs and symptoms, but more a set of underlying psychological mechanisms which can be expressed in varying ways.

Chapter 3

Post Traumatic Stress in the Dock

The judge looked me squarely up and down and called me to the witness box. After taking the oath I had to explain that I was a consultant clinical psychologist and Professor of Clinical Psychology, and that I had practised clinical psychology for thirty years. The barrister had told me to add that I had expertise in treating patients with Post Traumatic Stress Disorder. It was all quite strange and official but I just did as I was instructed. So far so good. I actually felt fairly confident about Mr Wainwright because not only had I initially assessed him for his solicitors and written a lengthy report, but I had also treated him for Post Traumatic Stress Disorder and got to know him well through that. He had responded like a dream to the therapy. His nightmares and flashbacks which had nearly driven him to despair had diminished week by week during the therapy until now – or to be more accurate a month before this court appearance when I had last seen him – and he was totally free of his "picture flashes" as he called them. So here I was, acting as an expert witness, in his case against the other driver's insurance company. They were claiming he had never experienced Post Traumatic Stress Disorder and they should not be liable for his loss of earnings, early retirement, and the costs associated with his treatment.

Dr Fish, the consultant psychiatrist working as an expert witness for the insurance company, would make his case after me. Mr Wainwright had been distressed by his interview with Dr Fish. "He made me feel as if I was a total liar and a hysteric," he explained in my next therapy session with him. "I've had more picture flashes in the last week, too," he added.

The judge then asked me to explain, taking my time, why I thought Mr Wainwright had Post Traumatic Stress Disorder. I had half prepared my answers and had spread a collection of papers in front of me.

"The starting point was that he experienced a trauma. Not just any trauma, but one with certain, defined characteristics. He was driving along the A337, which is a country road, quite leisurely, when a white Mercedes came over the brow of the hill at terrific speed on his side of the road. Mr Wainwright realized that a crash was inevitable but managed to swerve sufficiently to avoid a head-on collision. His car was hit in the rear right hand side and it rolled over many times before hitting a tree. Mr Wainwright and his work partner, Ben, both sustained injuries – Mr Wainwright to his head and shoulder and to his right leg, which was trapped by the collision with the tree. Ben, who was also injured, tried to pull him out but after several attempts had to leave him in the car and wait for the Fire Brigade to come."

I had rather expected the judge to intervene with questions, but he just listened patiently.

"What makes this important as far as Post Traumatic Stress is concerned is that it was a threat to his life. As he saw the Mercedes hurtling towards him so fast, he was convinced that he would die, and that he was powerless to protect himself. He said he felt a mixture of fear, panic, and horror at this moment, but was even more distressed when the car had stopped and he found that his leg, which had been broken in two places, was trapped. The pain was excruciating, but the main thing was that he saw smoke coming from the bonnet and screamed for Ben to pull him out. It was when he realized he was completely trapped and Ben had given up trying to get him out, that he totally panicked. He believed the car would burst into flames and that he would be burned alive."

"According to the police report," interjected the judge, rustling some papers in front of him, "it did not burst into flames, and the insurers claim there was little likelihood of that." This time I was quite surprised he had stopped me in my flow.

"Post Traumatic Stress does not depend so much on the objective degree of danger, but what the person truly believes about the danger. Mr Wainwright really expected the car to burst into flames. His terror was a response to his belief about the situation."

"All right, go on," replied the judge.

"So from the point of view of the American Psychiatric Association's

Diagnostic and Statistical Manual, he satisfied the first criterion for Post Traumatic Stress Disorder,[1] which is (and I had the quote ready in my papers):

'The person has been exposed to a traumatic event in which both of the following were present:

1. The person experienced, witnessed, or was confronted with an event that involved actual or threatened death or serious injury, or a threat to the physical integrity of self or others, and

2. The person's response involved intense fear, helplessness, or horror.'"

"Well, it seems to fulfil those criteria," the judge agreed. I had noticed a copy of the American Psychiatric Association's Diagnostic and Statistical Manual on his bench, so I was probably telling him what he knew already.

"What about the other criteria for Post Traumatic Stress Disorder?"

I started to feel a bit small now and that he was a step ahead of me. "The trauma is just the starting point," I continued. "It's the psychological reactions following the trauma that make up the disorder."

"Immediately after?"

"No, I'm referring to longer term. It's quite common for people to experience a range of disturbing symptoms straight after an accident, but these usually naturally subside. It's if the symptoms persist after…" – and here I double checked my copy of DSM open in front of me – "one month, and 'cause clinically significant distress or impairment', then PTSD, sorry, 'Post Traumatic Stress Disorder', can be diagnosed."

"We'll stick with PTSD; it's easier."

"There are three main psychological reactions which constitute PTSD. The first psychological process is re-experiencing the trauma. The memory won't seem to lie down or go away, but persistently intrudes into the person's consciousness against their will. Mr Wainwright experienced frightening flashbacks of the moment of impact and being trapped and seeing smoke. He described it as like 'watching a video – like a video that keeps going on and on'. It was not just that he replayed the trauma, but that the flashbacks suddenly erupted into his consciousness 'like a bolt out of the blue', along with a sudden 'sickening fear'. He also re-experienced the trauma in the form of nightmares of the crash or being burned alive."

"But there were no flames."

"The nightmares don't have to be direct replays but are often around the themes involved in the trauma."

I just remembered I had asked the barrister earlier how I should address the judge. "Your honour," he told me – and I had not offered a single "Your honour" so far – still he didn't seem too bothered. I continued.

"He re-experienced the trauma in other ways too. When he first got into a car after the accident he relived the whole experience, and he still finds it difficult to drive himself because it reminds him of the accident. Little triggers associated with the accident could instantly set off distress – traffic moving quickly or suddenly appearing around a bend; programmes about driving on TV, or even thoughts about fast driving could cause panicky reactions. Also once he trapped his finger in a door and couldn't understand why he felt real fear, until he worked out that it tapped into the idea of being trapped – as he had been in the accident. He can't go in lifts and will not lock toilet doors through the same sort of fear of being trapped. When he held the wheel his knuckles went white and he used to end up soaking with sweat."

"Used to? You said used to?"

"Yes. When I first saw Mr Wainwright it was to assess his condition only – that is documented in my first assessment report. At that time it was about eighteen months after the accident. He was having flashbacks three or four times a day and nightmares twice a week. About three months later he was referred back to me for Cognitive Behaviour Therapy, and so I saw him for a course of sessions which were successful in reducing his PTSD symptoms, Your Honour" (phew, I got it in).

"So he did have PTSD in May 2005, but not now?"

"Yes, that is right.

"The second main psychological reaction in PTSD is a physiological stress response – a physical over-arousal of the body. Mr Wainwright felt as if he was 'in overdrive' much of the day, which he likened to having had too many espressos. His over-arousal was almost unbearable while driving himself – eventually he employed a driver to drive him to work at the City of London. This over-arousal badly affected his sleep – previously he said he slept like a baby, but after the accident he found it incredibly difficult to drift off to sleep and awakened easily. His fear of having nightmares further impacted his sleep. Two of his most debilitating stress symptoms ultimately forced him to resign from his high-profile job in banking – he once prided himself on his good memory but after the accident was unable to remember names, numbers, and appointments, and even forgot the identity of major clients he had worked with for years. His concentration was 'shot', too – he just could not keep his mind on the task, forgot lines of argument, could not understand documents, or follow simple story lines in a movie. He gave in his notice before he made a serious error that might lose his bank millions of pounds. His colleagues noticed the change in him, too, and described him as changing from a 'Maserati to a moped'."

I took a brief look at the judge at this point to see whether he was frowning at my rather non-technical approach – but he seemed to be fine with it.

"The other aspect of this physiological stress response was his jumpiness. In the office he would visibly jump if the phone rang or the door opened suddenly. It became embarrassing for him and his colleagues.

"A third psychological mechanism that can be a part of PTSD relates to dissociation."

"Sorry, you've lost me there. What is dissociation?"

"It's when the mind automatically switches off if trauma is too unbearable – like being unable to remember the trauma, or feeling cut off or detached from usual emotions."

"Like a trip switch."

"Yes, something like that. Some psychologists think it is like a protective mechanism that shields the person from a trauma, but others say that the symptoms of dissociation are so frightening in their own right it is not so protective after all. The *Diagnostic and Statistical Manual* refers to this as 'numbing of general responsiveness'. It lists the following symptoms (here I referred to the open pages of DSM):

- *'Inability to recall an important aspect of the trauma*
- *Markedly diminished interest or participation in significant activities*
- *Feeling of detachment or estrangement from others*
- *Restricted range of affect (e.g. unable to have loving feelings)*

• *Sense of foreshortened future.'"*

"And did Mr Wainwright have these symptoms?" the judge asked.

"Only the sense of detachment. He noticed this in shops on a couple of occasions where he did not know what he was doing or why he was there. Once a man introduced himself to him at work. He said he watched his lips moving but didn't take anything in."

"So if he didn't have enough of this dissociation, does this mean Mr Wainwright did not have Post Traumatic Stress Disorder?" The fact that the judge had reverted to the full phrase "Post Traumatic Stress Disorder" alerted me to that fact that I was skating on thin ice. I couldn't really criticize the *Diagnostic and Statistical Manual* for including features like "diminished interest" as "numbing" because it might cast doubt on the reality of Post Traumatic Stress Disorder. Nor would it help to get into a debate about whether PTSD was a medical illness like pneumonia, with signs and symptoms, or simply a set of characteristics that have been observed frequently after a trauma.[2]

"It is possible to have Post Traumatic Stress Disorder without any features of dissociation. Perhaps I could go on to explain one more feature; it will be clearer," I suggested.

"Go on."

"I've explained that after a trauma, there are three different psychological reactions that together constitute 'Post Traumatic Stress Disorder' – reliving the experience, physiological stress response, and dissociation. They are all natural consequences of the trauma. These cannot be controlled by the person but are automatic reactions. There is a fourth factor that is more to do with a personality trait or the person's typical way of coping with distress – it is in the tendency to try to avoid thoughts, feelings, or conversations about the trauma. Some people will try hard not to think about the accident and not share it with those close to them, but rather keep a closed book. They may also try to avoid activities, people, or places that make them think about the accident. So Mr Wainwright avoided driving or watching anything about driving on TV. He felt unable to share what had happened with his wife, family, or work colleagues. It was actually Ben, his work partner, who was in the car with him, who explained the accident to the investment bank. At first he tried to avoid sleeping so that he wouldn't have nightmares and spent a lot of energy trying to distract himself or suppress the flashbacks, which was largely unsuccessful.

"So, although Mr Wainwright did not show many of the features of 'numbing of general responsiveness', he clearly did try to avoid reminders of the trauma. The *Diagnostic and Statistical Manual* puts avoidance and numbing under one heading so that a diagnosis of PTSD is possible if you have one or the other."

I felt as if I had been all around the houses and got a bit lost on the way.

"So you're saying that Mr Wainwright fulfils the criteria for PTSD because he had plenty of avoidance, but not much numbing? Is that right?"

"Yes, Your Honour."

"And you think the *Diagnostic and Statistical Manual* have got it wrong by lumping a personality trait in with a reaction to the trauma?" he summarized, showing more astuteness than I had reckoned on.

"Well, I didn't exactly say they were wrong."

"Well, I think you did. Thank you very much. We'll now adjourn for lunch and meet again at 2 p.m."

So, feeling a bit confused and wondering whether I had put my "psychologizing" before my client, I left the witness box.

Chapter 4

Why Me?

My name is Claire. I have been suffering from Post Traumatic Stress Disorder for about a year now, but until recently I didn't know that is what it was. I thought I was sinking into the worst sort of mental breakdown that there was and that I was getting more and more schizophrenic every day – until I found out about PTSD. I am having treatment for my condition now and have had four sessions with Dr Baker so far. Although I can see light at the end of the tunnel I am still far from well. The biggest comfort I have received from the sessions so far is to realize I am not mentally disintegrating, that this is a well-known psychological problem called Post Traumatic Stress Disorder that thousands of others suffer from. You don't know what a relief it is to realize that I am not insane.

In the third session Dr Baker asked me if I would like to write down what happened to me, and what Post Traumatic Stress Disorder felt like. He knew I had been keeping diaries of my illness and like to do bits and pieces of writing for the local papers and other things like that. He told me about the book he was writing on Post Traumatic Stress and how he really wanted people to understand it from the inside. He felt that listing all the symptoms and all that just didn't convey the problem properly to others. So he asked me to write down my experiences, referring back to my diaries, like a mini autobiography. He told me to write down whatever I wanted, not to bother what other people thought but to say what I thought was important. So I'm pleased to be able to share my annus horribilis with you, hoping it will benefit someone, and also by writing it down I will help my own recovery too.

Claire: Mother, Housewife, Person

I thought I would start off by telling you a bit about myself as a person, but even that is so difficult because what I was and what I am now is like two different people. The facts first; I am a mother with two children: Tom, aged twelve, and Anna, aged nine. They are wonderful children, but our life does seem like one round of dropping Tom off at scouts, karate, and orchestra and Anna at ballet, drama, and piano lessons plus all the sleep-ins with friends and so on. Phillip, my husband, is a very practical person – he's in charge of design software for a large engineering company. We met at university where I was studying English. I started off in full-time journalism but hated the pace of it, and having to do interviews with a mother whose daughter died in a car accident, or a couple whose soldier son had been shot in the Gulf war, which is funny because it's me who's had the accident now. I've sometimes wondered if it is some sort of punishment on me, but I realize that's silly. Ever since I left full-time employment, I have worked freelance doing articles and pieces on my first love, or what was my first love, recipes. There is a pretty good market for short articles on cooking... right now as I am writing this I should tell you that I've started to shake and go sweaty, just writing down the work "cooking".

The Worst Christmas Ever

[This is Dr Baker writing this section.] Claire came to our fifth session explaining that she had made a start on her narrative but realized she was not able to do the next section on "the worst Christmas ever" because she had found that even writing the word "cooking" had given her a flashback of her accident. I suggested that she forget about the whole exercise but she insisted that she had to do it even if it was for selfish reasons of "getting my head in order". So she asked me if I would write the section on her accident, based on what she had already told me, on the solicitor's letter and Dr Meyer's original assessment report. She would trust me to do it right and she could insert it into her narrative (without reading it) to give the full picture. Claire has rather understated her career as a freelance cookery writer and has not mentioned two cookery collections she has published, which is relevant because her accident has flattened her cooking career.

When Claire first came to see me she was accompanied by her mother, who did all the talking at first, until Claire gained some confidence, and thereafter did not have to rely on her mother. Her mother initially explained that they had come to see me because Claire had read my book *Emotional Processing: Healing Through Feeling*, which a friend had given her, and realized from it that she had not at all come to terms with her accident. When her mother had found out I lived nearby, she thought that this was almost like a sign that she should come to see me. Claire looked strangely puritanical in a dress with a very high neck and long sleeves – I didn't realize at this stage that this was to cover up her scars. This account is mainly based on what she told me in the first two sessions.

Her accident happened on 24 December 2006. She and her husband used to entertain extensively around Christmas and had invited a large group of friends and family for a special Christmas Eve meal, which involved three different types of bird stuffed inside each other. She had been cooking all day. She was working alone, the kitchen was very hot, and she had not stopped for a break for hours. Some fat from the cooking had spilled on the floor. She was holding a tray of roast potatoes in hot fat. As she turned around she slipped on the floor. She said she saw the tray of hot fat coming towards her face but managed somehow to keep it away, but in so doing it spilled down her shoulder and arm. In our treatment sessions she found it extremely difficult to continue the story and was sobbing a great deal from this point on. She saw the skin "drip off her arm" and smelled the appalling scent of her own burning flesh. She managed to get to the sink and hold her arm in cold water. She went to the accident and emergency department at the local hospital where the arm was examined and put in dressings. She had to go to hospital for more dressing the following day and thereafter was regularly taken to her doctor's surgery by her mother for three or four months for more dressings.

[This is Claire picking up the writing again.]

I suppose I don't have to elaborate too much on how this was the worst Christmas ever for me. It's coming round to Christmas soon and I dread the day now. My children tell me how much of a spoilsport I am.

The Kitchen

Since that Christmas Eve, which was nearly two years ago, I have tried to get back into my... I am reluctant to say the word, but have been practising it – "cooking", but I can't get past this oven thing. I just can't go near an oven. It makes me cringe. I tried to prepare some baked beans for Tom the other day – you couldn't get simpler than that. My heart started bumping, my hands shook, I got sweaty and hot. It's like pushing against an invisible barrier. You don't know how much trouble this has caused for the family. We've all got bigger because of the number of carry-outs we're eating, the children are always complaining about the number of salads and sandwiches we eat, although Phillip is very understanding. I've tried to work out the problem a bit – I know I'll have to face it at some point in my therapy – it's the heat bit that gets me. The feeling of heat coming off an oven just sets off those terrible flashbacks. I was on really strong painkillers for a long time after the accident and felt quite sleepy. It was when I eased off the painkillers that the flashbacks began. I can't eat or sleep for a long time after a flashback and am usually on the phone to Mum crying once again. And that's a really big change in me. I'm usually a strong person, bossy. Phillip says I am good at organizing things. It's as if I've become a child again, crying and having to run to Mum when things go wrong.

It's not just the kitchen that's the problem to me, but cuisine in general. It's supposed to be the love of my life – I dreamed of writing a famous cookbook, even of having my own show on the TV, and the collections of books on food I have collected over the years have to be seen to be believed. Guess where they are now – I had to get Phillip to put them up in the attic because I felt nauseous when I looked at them. I've not written a single article on food and even find myself switching over the TV channels if Jamie Oliver or something like that is on. Nine times out of ten I switch over to Nigella! It seems to be cooking wherever I look. I've certainly lost my culinary sparkle. I can't be bothered and what worries me is that this "can't be bothered-ness" is spreading out to other areas in my life.

I stopped entertaining, of course. We still get plenty of invites out for meals with our friends, but I find myself making excuses. I know I'm self-conscious about my arm but that's not the whole explanation – I often can't be bothered. If the BBC offered me a contract for "Claire's Culinary Secrets" I'm sure I would turn it down now. It sounds silly, but I often used to imagine picking up the mail from the doormat with the envelope marked "BBC". I never think like that now. My dreams have flown out of the window.

Claire, Hunchback of Notre Dame

It is "me" as a person that has taken a real dent from the accident. I used to feel quite attractive before – maybe a bit up and down. Sometimes I would think, "you're pretty damn attractive" and at other times "what a mess", but I was as positive as any woman could be about my looks. Phillip always praised me and seemed attracted quite a lot. I could fit into a size 10 and went clothes shopping a fair bit with my friend Lisa (Phillip didn't praise me for that!). Look at me now – I'm twelve and a half stone and look like a sack of potatoes. My arm is disgusting. This bit is really hard for me to write about, because I try never to think about my arm and never look at it. My wardrobe consists of four "frump" dresses. They cover up my arm and shoulder and are loose-fitting dresses because it is painful when the material touches my arm. So I've changed from Claire the pretty young housewife to Claire the Victorian nanny – an odd-looking Mary Poppins character. I feel embarrassed with others as if they are staring at my arm, which I know they're not really. I've cut right down on social outings, although Phillip and I still keep up our tennis (have you ever seen tennis players in long-sleeved blouses?). I've worked out this little routine where I can get up in the morning, get showered and dressed without catching sight of my arm. I have to keep my eyes shut in the shower. Phillip still says he is interested in me physically, but I can't believe anyone wants to make love to a disfigured creature. The other day we were watching a favourite drama series on TV, when I suddenly noticed that the leading lady had scars down her arm like me. I shuddered and couldn't bear to watch any more. She's very brave just to let it show like that. I'm afraid I'm light years from that. Maybe at the end of my therapy I'll be like her. I hope so.

The other thing, which I'm ashamed to talk about, is my temper. I can't understand it – I'm such a fun-loving, easygoing person. I never lose my temper, but now I'm touchy and prickly. Phillip gets it in the neck for little things that irritate me. I even shout at dear sweet Anna. I know it's me and not them. I try to control it but I keep telling them off. I feel so bad about it. How can an accident turn you into Mrs Grumpy overnight?

So, between my disfigured arm and disfigured personality I reckon Claire, the Hunchback of Notre Dame, is quite accurate.

The Dream World

After the accident I went into a sort of dream world. It was so weird and unusual that I knew it had to be part of my journal. The dream world has pretty much faded now, and this has given me the chance to try to analyse it and make sense of it.

Straight after the accident, when I was back and forth to the hospital it was a bit of a blank. I think I was in shock. My brain was numbed out. I didn't think of anything much, just went along with what Phillip and the nurses and doctors told me. After that I slipped into this dream world. At first I thought it was the effects of the heavy painkillers and tranquillizers that Dr Hedges, my General Practitioner, had given me, but I realized after a bit that this was something different. It's hard to describe what it was like. The closest thing that I can think of was that it was like being Alice in Wonderland. The world felt unreal, dreamy, and I was a bit of a detached onlooker. It wasn't quite a "déjà vu" experience, more that in some strange way everything was changed and different. For a long time I thought that this was schizophrenia and that the dream world was "me" disintegrating. Dr Hedges and Dr Baker had both told me this was quite a common mental state called "derealization", which I checked out on the Internet. It was a relief to know it was a temporary reaction and not the start of a long period of madness. I did a bit of psychology at university and reading about it did ring a few memory bells. Now I've come out of this dream world and have tried to work out why it happened. I've realized that before the accident I was travelling through life in a "safety bubble". I was safe, secure, and nothing could touch me. Accidents happened to "them" – people in the news – but that sort of thing doesn't happen to me. Every day flowed along nice and evenly, almost predictably, and would carry on like that forever. Then – wham! – along came this abomination that cannot and should not be happening to me, and my whole safety bubble is burst. So I think I entered my dream world because there wasn't any real world left any more. It's taken me time to adjust and get some stability back into my life again. My diaries are full of talk about "dream world", "unreality", "trance state", as I struggled to understand it and fend off schizophrenia. I knew it was crucial to escape from my dream world so it became a sort of obsession for me to puzzle it out. But this part at least is behind me now.

Why Me?

"Why me?" has been a question nagging away in the background, like an aching tooth. With all the people around me living, if not happy, then uneventful, lives, why did this disaster happen to me? It doesn't seem fair that with me being an attractive, young(ish) woman this should affect my looks so badly. And why now, when I'm in the prime of life, with a young family to look after – why not when I'm old and grey, with no one to look after any more? One day, when I caught myself actually saying, "Why me, why me, why me?" in quite a loud voice, I thought, "Who am I actually talking to? Whom is this question addressed to?" I realized that it was partly to myself but there was more to it than that. I was also talking to something bigger up there – nature, the heavens, to God possibly. The question really was, "Why, when you've made the world a fair place, would you pick on me for something like this?" I think I am quite a good person – kind to others, good tempered (usually but not now); we are members of our local church (though we don't go very often) and I believe in God, so why has this happened to me? I haven't done anything really evil that should deserve this, but it does feel like a punishment from whatever controls fate. The idea of the Greek gods chucking out thunderbolts from heaven that hit some poor unsuspecting soul fitted the picture more than a God of love who is looking after us. I felt picked on, singled out for punishment.

It was quite funny that at the time I was struggling with this that our vicar, Geoff, came to visit me. He's never been before but I think he must have got word of my accident from one of my friends. I was quite direct on tackling him on this "why me" question. I think I might have been a bit aggressive, as if it was his fault. He's a bit too evangelical for our taste, but very kind, and what he said stuck with me afterwards. He said that Jesus was asked something similar and referred to eighteen people who had been killed when a tower in Siloam had fallen on them. Jesus said they were no guiltier than any other people living in Jerusalem at the time. Geoff then asked me what the world would be like if God reversed the law of gravity every time a brick fell on someone from a roof, or stopped ice from being slippery when a car's wheels began to slip. This got me thinking afterwards about the way the world is made, and really to stop disasters, killings, and muggings we would have to be like Superman, able to defy gravity, catch bullets, resist incredible temperatures, and all the superhuman things he can do. If we could do all this, the world wouldn't be the same place – it would have a different set of laws. Although nowadays my emotional response is still "Why me?", the logic kicks in quite quickly and I say, "because the world is made the way it is". It doesn't help me when it comes to hot stoves, though. I feel that baking, ovens, and heating up food to boiling point is so incredibly dangerous. You won't get me near ovens for a long, long time.

Claire the Second, the New Me

I wanted to finish my "autobiography of an illness" on a positive note. Both Geoff and Dr Baker had said something that caught me by surprise. It was such a different way of thinking it was hard to get my head around. Up until recently I had seen this Post Traumatic Stress Disorder as a total flesh-eating disease, psychologically speaking. It has blighted my family life, hopes for a career, my looks, my weight, love life, sleep, and my personality. When Dr Baker said, "Can you think of anything positive that might result from your trauma?" I was amazed. He went on to describe "Post Traumatic Growth", in which new understandings and personal strengths might develop from the tragedy. He mentioned some people who had been through the 9/11 disaster who no longer "fretted at the small stuff" and realized the value of their close relationships with their loved ones more and more.

At the moment I am having difficulty seeing anything positive about the situation. I am optimistic about the results of therapy – I think that in time I will find new ways to overcome the illness. But on the negative side, if the accident hadn't happened I wouldn't need therapy now. I suppose I do feel a bit closer to Phillip and realize what a rock he is when things go wrong like this. But the huge issue I just can't live with are the reminders of what happened. I'm reluctant to write the word "flashback" because it might get me thinking about the accident, and then bingo, set me off. But they, and my dreams about the accident, are like huge boulders standing in the way of recovery.

I have written this journal over the last week, adding bits and pieces and occasionally checking back to the diaries I wrote earlier. Writing this has been a positive experience for me – apart from the first hiccup when I couldn't write about the accident myself. It has made my thinking clearer and at times given me a sense of release. Apart from that first hiccup I think that writing this diary has reduced my flashbacks. But there is no getting round the terror which flashbacks strike into me. Terror is the right word because they are like a poisoned cake with all the most shocking ingredients mixed in together, ready to kill off the victim. I need to say this bit, but it is hard for me. All of a sudden, out of the blue, with no warning at all, I relive that terrible moment. In my mind I see it so vividly. I smell what I smelled at the time, and I feel the pain again. How can I live life to the full if I can be suddenly struck with the same tragedy again and again? I try and I try to block these fatal reminiscences and I try to stop my nightmares too, but it's like the Hound of Hell pursuing me night and day.

I had to explain how bad this is, because it is impossible to understand the terror if you haven't had a flashback yourself. I hope that by writing this I can help someone else struggling like me with the dreadful aftermath of their trauma. I have purposely left flashbacks until last because that was the hardest bit to write, but there, I have written it now, and I hope it helps everyone understand this curse a little better.

The Psychology Behind PTSD

Chapter 5

Emotional Processing

This is the story of a man who was given a casket. It looked a bit like a small treasure chest made of hardened brown leather with carvings over it that gave it a sinister air. As soon as he took it he realized his mistake; a powerful repulsive smell emanated from the casket. It was hardly a casket of treasure, more a casket of horrors. His instantaneous reaction was to give it back, but the "benefactor" had gone. He had once put a broken garden chair in his recyclable waste bin and had it returned by the refuse collectors with a rude note, so he was pretty sure that he couldn't get away with passing it off as household or garden refuse. So he was stuck with it.

At first he covered it with old towels and blankets to stifle the smell, but it seemed to haunt him wherever he went. He tried closing the casket more tightly, spraying it with aftershave, and eventually put it on the compost heap at the bottom of the garden. But still the smell seemed to penetrate at the oddest of times, waking him from sleep and spoiling his meals. Eventually he dug a hole and buried it. Even then it seemed to have a presence of its own; he could not get the appalling smell out of his mind.

He said to himself, "I've always got over things like this in the past. I just need to forget it." And he tried very hard to forget. Although no one had actually told him what was in the casket, he had a notion at the back of his mind that it contained a material so toxic that if opened, it would destroy him and his neighbourhood. He harboured other thoughts too: if he were to open the casket, it could do untold damage to his lungs, reek the house out so that it would never smell fresh again; that the casket could never be closed once opened, and the stench would go on and on forever. It seemed that the smell had a life of its own, pursuing him whatever he did.

He decided to talk to his friend Sammy about it. After listening to his story, Sammy came up with a proposal he had not considered. "Why not just open the casket, see what's inside, and let it air out?" "Supposing it's dangerous. Supposing it kills me. What if I unleash some terrible power that can never be stopped?" Sammy's smile told him he was a bit over the top. "Well, nothing you have done so far has worked," replied Sammy.

He thought this over for a few days and then decided to take the risk and follow Sammy's advice. It took him a few more days to pluck up the courage to actually dig up the casket. Wearing an overcoat, gloves, goggles, and with a scarf muffled around his nose and mouth he eventually and with great trepidation prised open the casket.

It was everything he feared; the smell was so appalling he was filled with fear and felt overwhelmingly nauseous. He was tempted to close the casket and bury it again, when Sammy appeared around the corner a bit late for the "grand opening day", encouraging him to "hang in there". From a good distance he did hang in there, keeping an anxious eye on the casket lest something rather horrid might come out of it. He had vague memories of the film Alien, where unspeakable things could crawl out of unseen hiding places. But nothing did, and after a bit he began chatting with Sammy. It was about twenty minutes later that he realized for the first time that, far from the expectation of an ever-increasing stench, it was less pungent now. As it got weaker over the next half hour he asked Sammy whether they should go and look at the contents. Sammy was all for it – so gingerly the couple approached the casket and peered inside. It was perfectly disgusting and he wanted to withdraw, but Sammy again encouraged him to "tough it out". He noticed the unpleasant colours, textures, and the point from which the smell seemed to emanate most powerfully. He noticed it was smaller than he thought. He had the sense it was getting smaller as it was exposed to the air, but he wasn't sure. "Let's close it and come back tomorrow," suggested Sammy.

Every day, from then on, he opened the casket and left it open all day. It was usually worst when he first opened it, but during the day the penetrating smell no longer seemed to haunt him in the same way. He never liked that box and was always somewhat suspicious of it, but it ceased to trouble him, and apart from the odd reminder he forgot about it. He simply left it open at the bottom of his garden.

He wished he had never met the man who gave him the casket, but that was in the past now.

Nature's Second Immune System

These next chapters take a different perspective. Up to this point I have been able to illustrate aspects of Post Traumatic Stress using case histories of real people, which helps to bring the problems to life. The next few chapters, however, are much more to do with the psychological theory – questions relating to how we store and recall traumatic memories, what emotional processing consists of, and how therapy helps in the emotional processing of the traumatic memory. In this little story about the man and his casket, I've tried to sketch out some of the psychological dimensions underlying Post Traumatic Stress Disorder. The story is really about a traumatic incident coming into a person's life and how to deal with the distressing memories of the trauma, characterized in the story by an awful smell.

We are all familiar with the body's immune system, which consists of an amazingly complex sequence of biochemical reactions designed to protect us from the harmful effects of invading viruses and bacteria. The immune system is like a second system of defence, a type of back up. Our bodies are made in such a way that the inner organs are protected by skin and bone, which are amazingly resilient. For example, the brain, an organ that is essential to life, has a thick protective skull and no easy entrance points for invading organisms. The body is designed to minimize damage and is our first line of defence and protection. If invasive organisms do penetrate the first line of defence, we have a second line of defence: our immune system. This system is ready to smother, absorb, convert, and generally nullify invading organisms. It doesn't stop an organism invading in the first place. However, it does subdue it if invasion should occur.

Human beings are also equipped with a type of emotional immune system.[1] It is not concerned with assault from physical material such as bacteria and viruses, but with emotional assault. This emotional processing system does not stop emotional hurts, stresses, and traumas happening, but it is designed to absorb, minimize, and transform emotional assaults in order to keep us psychologically healthy. In this sense it is similar to the body's immune system, which protects us from physical damage and ultimately death. The emotional processing system protects us from psychological damage and ultimately mental breakdown.

The term "emotional processing" was first introduced by the psychologist Jack Rachman in 1980.[2] He defined emotional processing as "a process whereby emotional disturbances are absorbed, and decline to the extent that other experiences and behaviour can proceed without disruption". To grasp the significance of this, imagine someone who was criticized at work. What would happen if, for instance, the feeling of being upset about the incident did not decline? It would mean that the person would remain permanently aroused and upset for life! For Rachman, the evidence that the emotional event had been satisfactorily absorbed or "processed" was that the person was able to resume their normal everyday activities without being disrupted by the effects of the emotional event. The disruption includes preoccupation with the event – gnawing on it like a bone, having intrusive thoughts or dreams about it, or little triggers re-awakening thoughts and feelings about it. In other words the event keeps reappearing in one guise or another. Other less direct signs of unprocessed emotional disturbance described by Rachman are heightened arousal, strong or persistent negative emotions, agitation, poor concentration, or lapses in memory. If an emotional event has not been properly emotionally processed we know about this both from our thoughts and our state of feeling, disrupting a normal and easy flow of experience and the ability to concentrate on the daily issues of life.

Processing Deep Hurts

A good example of emotional processing can be found in one almost universal cause of emotional distress – the death of a loved one. There are few who escape this unfortunate distress during their lifetime. So far I have been referring to comparatively minor "emotional events". The death of someone close usually has a greater and more significant impact but the theory is the same, even if the emotional event is much greater. The death of someone close means there is much more emotionally distressing material to process than for a critical remark.

At first the person may feel shock, unbelief, or numbed at the death of their loved one. "There must be some mistake – can't they be resuscitated?" As the unpalatable truth begins to dawn, waves of grief cascade so that it becomes emotionally overwhelming. Thoughts of the loved one and their death continually press into consciousness with accompanying feelings of sadness. The person may sob and cry for long periods of time. Sometimes the tears may bring respite, but further reminders of the deceased set off the whole process again. One could say that initially the person is immersed in their loss from both a cognitive perspective (thoughts of the person, memories, reminders) and an emotional perspective (grief, sadness, tears). The concerns of daily life and being able to concentrate on everyday activities are swamped by the overwhelming onslaught of thoughts, memories, and emotions.

Sometimes by a great act of will relatives have to put aside their grief and concentrate on the concerns of everyday life – arranging the funeral and flowers and informing family – but the emotional distress cannot be easily forgotten. The person may lose interest in food and even sleep may desert them. They may endlessly talk with others and go over the same concerns – having friends and family around with the same loss enables mutual sharing and mutual tears. The funeral itself, which might come after a week or so of intense grieving, is both a formal occasion to say goodbye to the loved one and an informal occasion to talk with others about them. After the funeral and the family gathering are over and all have gone home, the person is left with many months of tussling with memories and emotions about the loved one. It takes a long time to accept the loss and adapt to a new way of living without the loved one around. Episodes of crying may still occur but they may become sporadic. Other thoughts and plans begin to be taken up, interspersed with the memory of the loved one. Gradually the activities of daily life become uppermost in the person's mind and concern with the memories of the loved one more like oases of grief. Over time the person is able to think about the loved one, talk about them, see reminders of them in photos without being overwhelmed with such powerful emotions. At this stage we could say that they have finally processed the distressing emotional event. The journey may have had many ups and downs, but a day is reached when the powerful emotional memories have lost their power, and do not disrupt the person's consciousness to such an extent that they cannot get on with the tasks of life.

I have painted a picture here of successful emotional processing

– where powerful emotional distress has been accommodated or transformed. But emotional processing can be seriously hindered. Not everyone allows emotional processing to take its course. In Chapter 2, Mrs E., who could not believe that her son Alan, "the light of her life", had died, erected a sort of living memorial to her son. She had not allowed herself to step on the first rung of the ladder of grief. Emotional processing had hardly begun for her.

I said earlier that emotional processing was like a second immune system, an emotional immune system. In the physical immune system everything happens automatically – a person has no control over whether killer cells and macrophages attack and engulf invading viruses. The body does it! Although emotions are in part automatic functions, they are nothing like as automatic as cellular biochemical processes involved in the physical immune system. People have attitudes towards their own emotions and can, for instance, stifle tears, suppress feelings of grief, and distract themselves from memories of their loved one.[3] Human beings are capable of erecting many defences, which can disrupt and hinder what would otherwise be a fairly automatic grief process.[4] So when we are considering emotional processing we are often talking about disrupted or faulty emotional processing.[5] When individuals do not know or trust their own emotions, or try to force their emotions in a particular direction, they might stifle their own protective emotional immune system.

Why emotional processing is so relevant to PTSD is that it provides an understanding of how normal individuals deal with, absorb, or "process" difficult and disturbing emotional events in their life.[6, 7, 8] The underlying assumption made by Rachman was that "most people successfully process the overwhelming number of emotional events in their life".

Understanding how emotional processing works in normal healthy individuals will help us to understand:
- how PTSD starts
- why some people develop PTSD and others don't
- how to make our emotional life more healthy and
- how to reduce the impact of a trauma if it does happen, thus providing a degree of protection or "immunization".

The Trauma

We have looked at a small emotional event – the upset of being criticized at work. We have also looked at a more significant event – the death of a loved one. Let us now turn to trauma. Although trauma is another example of an emotional event it has a number of features that stretch our emotional processing capacity to the uttermost.[9, 10]

A trauma is an unusually shocking event for a person that hopefully happens quite rarely, maybe once in a lifetime. Different traumas can have different effects, so let's try to understand the different categories of trauma and their varied effects.

1. Personal accidents. This includes car crashes, fires, drowning, and accidents at home or at work, generally involving danger to one's own life, or seeing others harmed. PTSD can develop regardless of whether someone sustained an injury. Some individuals can develop PTSD when there has been no physical injury, and others do not develop PTSD even though they have been injured. If an accident does involve personal injury or disability the emotional aftermath is usually more complex, and hospital visits, specialist consultations, surgery, compensation claims, and court hearings can unduly prolong and inflame psychological suffering.

2. Large-scale accidents. These happen to larger groups of people, such as the Piper Alpha oilrig explosion in Scotland, London's King's Cross station fire, or the Chernobyl nuclear power disaster.

3. Intentional disasters. These are large-scale accidents caused intentionally, such as the 9/11 attacks, IRA bombings in Ireland, or ETA bombings in Spain. The end result may be similar to a large-scale accident, but for individuals trying to come to terms with the trauma the fact that a human being intended them harm introduces perplexing emotive elements.

4. Natural disasters. These can include volcanic eruptions, floods, tornados, forest fires, and tsunamis. Trauma therapists have assumed natural disasters are easier to recover from than man-made ones, because no one can be blamed. Others have claimed that even natural disasters are not devoid of a

human element, and blame can still be attributed to human sources – "Why weren't we warned about the impending eruption?" "Why did they build houses on the flood plains?" Sometimes this involves self-blame or guilt – "Sooner or later an earthquake was bound to happen – why didn't I move from this place earlier?" "I shouldn't have put my family through this."

5. Personally inflicted crimes. These include muggings, thefts, gun wounds, stabbings, and kidnappings. These are like personal accidents but involve another human being purposely inflicting harm.

6. Sexual abuse. This category of trauma has many elements of personally inflicted crimes, but the sexual element often adds extra disturbing personal features. Sexual abuse is often targeted at children, may be perpetrated by those who ought to be protecting them, may be repeated over long periods of time, and recovery is often prevented by the abuser pressuring the child to keep it secret. This also includes rape, sexual abuse, and physical abuse in marital relationships.

7. Illness-related. This can include receiving a diagnosis of a serious disease, having a sudden attack such as a heart attack, the pain and disability involved in a disease, the trauma of medical interventions or seeing loved ones die or suffer. The risk of developing PTSD may vary with the physical proximity of the trauma – for instance seeing a loved one suffer usually has a greater impact than hearing of the suffering of relatives from a distance.

8. Wartime combat. Obviously being involved in a war exponentially increases the risk to service personnel of being harmed, or seeing others maimed and killed. What may make this different from a personal accident is that danger is more predictable in the sense that death and injuries are an inevitable consequence of war. There may be an element of preparation and partial stress inoculation in the training of troops and the psychologically protective effect of working in a unit. Non-service personnel can be caught up in war too, such as journalists and civilian refugees, for whom the trauma may present different elements, such as helplessness,

unpredictability, and lack of a protective support group, so it is often worse for them than for service personnel.

9. Long-term or repeated trauma. Concentration camp inmates, those being systematically tortured, or people targeted for genocide experience trauma in which pain, maiming, rape, separation from loved ones, personal danger, and seeing dead bodies can be a daily occurrence. The accumulated onslaught of so many different traumas can be devastating.

In summary, what makes a trauma traumatic?
- how severe it was
- whether it was prolonged
- whether it was repeated
- how personal it was
- whether it occurred to you or to others
- physical closeness to the trauma
- personal differences in the way that different individuals interpret the trauma and whether it echoes previous psychological distress
- whether it was expected
- the amount of group support or training prior to the trauma
- whether the person has suffered trauma in the past.[11]

There is another part to the story, though. A traumatic event usually happens only once – there are some exceptions to this such as torture, genocide, or childhood sexual abuse – but by and large a trauma is a one-off experience. Yet Post Traumatic Stress Disorder may last many years. We need something else in the equation to understand how one event can reverberate so long in the human emotions. That is why we need to understand more about memory, the way in which the trauma is stored in the mind.

Chapter 6

Burying the Memories

Many traumas, such as a car accident or disaster, occur only once. What has a continuing effect on the person is the memory of the trauma. It can be replayed in the mind hundreds of times, so that in effect the trauma is relived many times. The memory of the trauma may differ from ordinary memories in being incredibly vivid, almost like a replay of the original event. The scene may be remembered in acute detail, involving several senses. The person may hold a vivid record of each millisecond with video-like visual memory and a memory of sounds, smells, bodily sensations, pain, and the recurrence of the emotions felt at the time. For one man the bodily feeling and "popping" sound of his leg as it broke was the focal part of his traumatic memory. The most distressing second can usually be remembered especially accurately.

Normally memories can be recalled at will or little reminders may spark them off. After a trauma the memories seem to have a will of their own, erupting when least expected, and with much power and emotion.[1] In the normal course of recovery, when the person does not develop PTSD, the powerful emotion associated with the memory will naturally decrease as the weeks go by.[2] One of the cardinal features distinguishing PTSD is that the memory continues to intrude over months and does not seem to naturally fade. The memories can recur as flashbacks during the day or as nightmares at night.

"Hot memories" is a term used by psychologists to describe what happens when a powerful emotional event is stored in memory.[3] The way in which it is laid down in memory differs from the ordinary "cold memories" of everyday life, which are not invested with such emotional significance. Nearly everybody can tell you what they were doing when they heard about Princess Diana's death or the 9/11 disaster. The emotional power and shock of the event causes this type of memory to be given priority. If I were to ask you to recall what you were doing one week before Diana's death it would be much harder to do.

It is not just that significant memories are given priority in the memory system, but leading psychologists propose that emotional memories are stored in a unique way.

In the same way that computer software programs are written in machine code, a simple mathematical language that governs how the program operates, memories are stored in the brain in a code system too. Seymour Epstein, a senior psychologist who worked at the University of Massachusetts, defined two different types of code system: "We apprehend reality by two conceptual systems that operate in parallel; an automatic, experiential system (emotions) and an analytic, rational system (thought), each operating by its own rules of inference."[4]

Wilma Bucci, Professor of Psychoanalysis at Adelphi University, actually refers to this as a "multiple code" theory.[5] The code system closest to logic and language, which she calls a "symbolic system", is stored in a more tightly organized cohesive way in certain areas of the brain. This involves "single channel" sequential processing code; in other words, we can only attend to one train of thought at a time, which unfolds along a time line. There is a different code system underlying emotion. It is a multiple channel set-up much closer to the senses, including smell, hearing rhythms, pitch, physical sensations in the body, sense of movement, balance, and touch.[6] This information is stored in a more dispersed way in the brain, in a similar way to how information from the senses is stored. For instance, in walking, the head, legs, and feet are automatically synchronized, and the rapidly changing visual scenes as one walks along are calculated by the brain as one seamless experience. It is an automatic, continuous, intuitive, multi-channel system of processing.[7, 8, 9]

In Post Traumatic Stress, the crucial feature is how such memories are retrieved. Memories stored in the symbolic or "rational" system are accessed much more easily and are much more under voluntary control – we might not be able to remember everything that was said in a conversation but we know where we are looking and how to get hold of that memory. Psychologist Chris Brewin actually refers to this as "Verbally Accessible Memory" (VAM).[10] Events, facts, and ideas are all part of Verbally Accessible Memory and can be consciously and mentally recalled, giving us a sense of mental control. He refers to emotional memories as "Situationally Accessible Memory" (SAM), which are not so consciously or verbally accessible but are "situationally accessible", that is, we can get at such memories by situations (going back to the scene of the crash), little reminders (e.g. seeing ER on TV), smells, sounds, similar movements as in the accident, and so on. In other words associated stimuli can evoke a memory rather than rational (symbolic) thought. So attempts to consciously control our mental life may be successful in the realm of rational ideas but are fairly useless in controlling traumatic memories. Yet chance little triggers – a smell of smoke or the sound of squealing tyres, can set off a whole chain of memory. This provides many "secrets" for unlocking emotional memories and it is possible to harness this to the full in Emotional Processing Therapy.

We have been talking about attempts to recall memories, but now let us turn to attempts to block out memories.

Dissociation: Unconscious Control of Emotional Pain

There are two main psychological mechanisms that block memories, an automatic cut-off system, referred to as dissociation, and consciously controlled strategies for mentally controlling memories.[11, 12]

Dissociation represents a distinct psychological mechanism in which the memory is stored intact, but the mind automatically and unconsciously blanks out part or all of the memory so that it cannot be easily recalled. We know that the memory is laid down intact because people with memory blocks can later recall the blocked-off memories. Traditionally this has been regarded as a protective mental device to shield the person from the appalling memories and thus reduce the psychological distress. Often this is not an entire effect in which the whole memory is blocked out, but a partial effect – parts of the memory can be recalled but others seem to be missing.

Here are some of the telltale signs that dissociation is occurring:
- Derealization – the world seems strange, different, or surreal.

- Depersonalization – something about "me as a person" seems unreal or different.
- Dreamlike state or trance – attention may be focused much more narrowly (like hypnosis) and information about the wider world missed.
- Out of body experience – seeming detached or almost as if objectively watching oneself.
- Feeling detached from others.
- Feeling numb, a "block" or a "blank".
- Feeling as if it is happening to someone else and not to me.
- Inability to feel emotions, or not feel them as strongly as normally.

This automatic dissociation should be distinguished from conscious efforts by the person to avoid thoughts, memories, and reminders of the trauma. It is thought that many of these really powerful and unusual experiences listed above are due to the huge investment of mental energy in separating the memory from consciousness in this way. The mind is trying to remove something from consciousness, and so it is not surprising that many of the feelings, such as a dreamlike state, are changes in the feeling of consciousness.

The Curtains are Drawing Back

Dissociation is not something you see every day, even as a clinician. Vivian, an extremely articulate lady, who was recovering from breast cancer, was coming to see me and my co-therapist Lin, a cancer specialist nurse, for help with Post Traumatic Stress symptoms resulting from the trauma of cancer. In the therapy session I am about to describe we had to change the venue from a rather plush office suite to the interview room in "Ward 16", the cancer treatment ward where she had received her chemotherapy. It was the only office available. As I was walking past the patient waiting area on the ward just before the session, I noticed Vivian had tears in her eyes, so quickly bundled her into the interview room. "What's wrong?" I asked.

She explained, "When I walked into the ward I saw all the familiar sights, staff I recognized, beeping noises. It all came flooding back, exactly how I used to feel, the anxiety. The ward had felt like a safe haven after my last chemo. The episode was closed; so this was like re-opening it."

She said she felt very strange and explained her experience in detail. What she was describing was a dissociation experience in which her painful emotions were cut off from her normal state of consciousness. "My body feels numb as if my head and body were separate. It is almost as if I am out of the room. I can hear your questions but they feel like they are at a distance. It's quite hard to bring myself to answer."

"Would you like to cancel the session and leave it for another day, because today's session was going to be about facing the memories of your chemo, which is about as hard as you could get?"

No, she was determined she wanted to continue despite feeling so odd. Her experience was obviously quite powerful, but she didn't look detached in any way and seemed to be responding normally to my questions. We continued to discuss her memories of the chemotherapy. After about fifteen minutes, she interjected, "The curtains are drawing back."

"Could you explain that to me?" I asked.

"Yes, suddenly objects in the room have become real again and I felt as if I was returning to normal. As soon as it became real, I felt anxiety sensations in the pit of my tummy."

At this point, Lin, my co-therapist, started to talk about endorphins, and Vivian did admit that when she felt "numb", it was like being quite high, as if on drugs, "quite good in a way". We went on in the session to discuss some quite emotive elements in her chemotherapy when she had been tempted to give up the chemotherapy altogether. She faced these memories full on, as she had been determined to do in the previous session, and the dissociation experience did not recur.

What Vivian described was a dissociative episode in which the pain of her memories of chemotherapy was anaesthetized or detached from her normal consciousness. At the moment the numbness switched off, she was able to feel anxiety again, but she stuck with it and was able to describe some painful but significant memories, which contributed towards her psychological recovery. This illustration provides a bit of background for understanding the way in which dissociation removes emotional pain.

Distraction, Avoidance and Suppression: Conscious Control of Emotional Pain

If a trauma has been particularly distressing it is not surprising that some people will try to minimize painful memories about it. Different people use different strategies to control memories. Some strategies resemble mental gymnastics, but others are more practical, such as avoiding activities or places.[13, 14, 15]

Distraction

In distraction, whenever the first signs of an impending disturbing memory occur, the person does something to distract themselves. This includes turning their attention elsewhere by switching on the TV, playing music, doing mental arithmetic, talking to someone, or going out. To some extent distraction is a normal human activity, but it depends on the degree of mental effort involved. It becomes a problem when the person needs to distract themselves regularly throughout the day. Clinical psychology has sometimes been complicit in teaching patients sophisticated distraction techniques such as imagining oneself on the beach, or pinging an elastic band on one's wrist when a distressing thought occurs – well, maybe not so sophisticated after all! The aim of distraction is to avoid experiencing the powerful emotions associated with the memory of the trauma.[16]

Behavioural Avoidance

Often, the person tries to avoid all the "situational cues" around the accident. They may avoid driving or going anywhere near the scene of the trauma, or they may even avoid watching similar accidents on the TV or movies. They are usually trying to avoid the key elements that occurred in their own accident because these are the most distressing.[17]

Social Avoidance

Social avoidance can reach extreme lengths. This may include trying to avoid any conversation that might be related to the trauma. While it is relatively easy to control one's own conversation, the conversation of others is problematic. Perhaps it is easier when family and close friends are concerned – they know about the trauma and may "tiptoe" around the topic for fear of upsetting the person. Trying to avoid the topic may put quite a pressure on those closest to the person. Sometimes the sufferer attempts to "steer" conversations, keeping others well off the topic of the trauma. Many subtle and ingenious conversational ploys can develop. Sometimes the person simply starts to avoid conversations and close down contact with others, paradoxically reducing the social support network which is so important in combating PTSD.

Suppression of Emotional Feeling

In suppression, the person may not try to stop reminders of the accident but does try to squash or control the emotional feeling evoked by the memory. "Bottling up emotions", "smothering feelings", or "sweeping them under the carpet" are typical phrases that people use about their efforts to control the experience of emotions. One woman said, "I feel butterflies in my tummy and feel I want to cry. Then I suppress my feelings. I take a great big breath, hold it in, tense myself, or put my mind on to something else – take the dog out for a walk, do the housework. I say 'Don't be so stupid; pull yourself together.'" In this example she is not only trying to squash the experience of having an unpleasant emotion, but also distracting her mind by taking the dog for a walk, or by doing housework.[18]

Often techniques of distraction, avoidance, and suppression may merge together or form combinations unique to an individual. Sometimes a complex labyrinth of defences ensures the memory is effectively immobilized and imprisoned. Chemical suppression – the use of drugs such as antidepressants, tranquillizers, and sleeping tablets, or self-medication in the form of alcohol, soft and hard drugs – is a frequently chosen method for controlling unpleasant emotional feelings.

A Psychological Model of Traumatic Memories

Figure 1 (overleaf) illustrates these ideas about conscious and unconscious memories. How the memory is stored after a trauma forms the first part of emotional processing. The diagram distinguishes between the storage of the memory of the trauma from the memory recall, when it enters conscious awareness. Dissociation is the emotional mechanism by which the memories remain in "deep storage" and are not consciously recalled. The "emotion

Figure 1. Storing traumatic memories

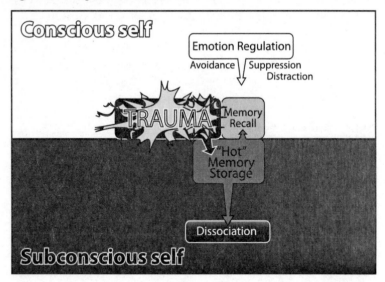

regulation" box is placed within the "conscious self" section – this is to say that avoidance, distraction, and suppression are things that the person does to try to keep the memory recall at bay. When I say the person consciously uses these regulation techniques it sounds very contrived, as if they've planned it and are purposely using the strategy. Actually they may only be dimly aware that this is what they are doing, but I wanted to distinguish it from dissociation, which is much more automatic. Emotion regulation strategies are not designed to control all memories – the person might not try to control memories of a pleasant family holiday that kept popping into their mind. It is the unpleasant memories of the trauma that are kept at bay. The memory is charged with much of the emotional power of the original trauma. Horror, fear, and loss of control may all be bound up in the memory. The attempt to control the memory is really an attempt to not feel the appalling emotions.

A Key Understanding

The crucial part of all these attempts to control mental states, whether it is unconscious "dissociation" of the memory of the trauma, or conscious strategies, is to effectively keep the memory contained. This blocks the natural process of recovery, not allowing emotional processing to proceed. While this may not matter in the short term, if it develops as a permanent coping strategy it will not allow any emotional processing of the traumatic memory. Traumatic memories don't fade with time if kept in the dark. The memories will remain as powerful as ever and continue to surface as flashbacks and nightmares. The memory must be accessed at an emotional level to enable emotional processing to start. Intellectual discussion just will not do – it is the powerful emotional nexus of memories that needs to be accessed.

Recognizing a blockage in the emotional processing of the traumatic memory is the key to understanding why the symptoms of PTSD develop. Encouraging the emotional processing of the memories is the key to therapy for PTSD.

Chapter 7

Emotions, the Stuff of Life

Every Christmas our family, like millions of others around the world, watch Frank Capra's classic film *It's a Wonderful Life*. This Christmas I humoured my daughter who put on the DVD, but I really felt, "I've seen this so many times it will just be a drag." But sure enough, come the emotional scenes as George Bailey (James Stewart) realizes what a wonderful life he has, I'm snivelling and sobbing with the best of them. Isn't it strange how some things touch the heart and move us? Movies aren't just about moving pictures but the moving landscapes of our heart too. They can elicit righteous indignation, excitement, fear, humour, a sense of wrongs righted, curiosity, and anticipation. A film can spark off a whole spectrum of different emotions, ranging from the simple reactions to a cartoon to the more complex constellations of an Oscar-winning classic. In films like *It's a Wonderful Life* the emotional pull may be a little more obvious than in other movies, but emotions do not have to be powerful to be emotions. Smaller nuances of rapidly changing feelings are still emotions – it is maybe harder to label them "sadness" and "joy" but nonetheless they are still "affective states", as a psychologist might say. Movies are of course a crystallized and kaleidoscopic version of life, exaggerated to appeal to us and condensed into one hour forty minutes. Without the capacity to experience emotional tones and meanings I doubt whether movies and novels could hold any appeal at all.

I have in mind reading an Agatha Christie thriller – in a good thriller the emotional tone will be one of suspense – waiting for the unfolding of the mystery set in the early chapters, but with other elements such as surprise, confusion, and resolution. But someone might say, "There is no emotion at all in reading a science book." Compared to a thriller I suppose that is right – it's predominately an intellectual pursuit, but nonetheless emotional tones of a different kind may be present, such as the satisfaction involved in intellectual curiosity, finding out new things, feeling of mastery over subject matter, or dissatisfaction about the arguments used. The point I am making is that although movies and novels are condensed versions of life, heightening emotional feeling, in real life we have the capacity to feel a whole palette of emotional experience. Perhaps when we think of emotions, what come to mind are the stronger, simple emotions of personally significant events, such as grief at the death of a relative, but "emotional experience" is present in some way or another most of the time.

Here are some of the different dimensions of emotions. Examples of the qualities of emotions are on the left, and examples showing contrasting qualities are on the right.

Positive (e.g. excited)	Negative (e.g. depressed)
Strongly felt (e.g. anger)	Weakly felt (e.g. slight sympathy)
Mixtures of negative emotions (e.g. a combined feeling of grief, anger, and dissatisfaction)	Single emotion (e.g. disgust)
Mixtures of positive and negative emotions (e.g. unrequited love)	Single emotion (e.g. sexual desire)
Subtle (e.g. happiness at family being together at Christmas being combined with the realization that it won't last for long and a desire to make the most of it but realizing that trying too hard might spoil the moment)	Simple (e.g. fear)
Sudden (e.g. temper)	Gradual build-up (e.g. stress)
Sporadic (e.g. laughing at a comedian)	Continuous (e.g. resentment)
Rapidly changing emotions (e.g. ups and downs of feelings watching your favourite football team)	Relatively stable (e.g. contentment)

Personally related to me (e.g. grief at break-up of relationship)	Not related to me (e.g. slight sadness at hearing about the break-up of the relationship of a friend)
Relevant to your own emotion schemas (hang-ups) (e.g. small separation experiences causing strong reactions)	Not related to one's emotion schemas (e.g. separation causes an appropriate level of feeling)
Infrequently experienced (e.g. falling in love)	Frequently experienced (e.g. background feeling of being alive)

Time Line of Emotional Experience

Past oriented (e.g. nostalgia)	Present oriented (e.g. enjoyment of having a family meal)	Future oriented (e.g. anticipation of a holiday)

When one considers these different dimensions it can be seen that emotional experience is a varied and important aspect of living; emotions give life colour and spice.[1, 2, 3, 4]

The Barometer of Life

In the same way that our emotional feelings are the response to the unfolding situations in a movie, our own emotional feelings are the response to what is happening in our life. They provide us with personally felt feedback. In a sense they are the barometer of our life.[5] A movie may be packaged a little more neatly than our own life and the plot is easier to fathom, but nevertheless our emotions reflect the unfolding situations in our own life. There is one difference, though. A movie pretty much tells us how to appraise the events that unfold. It is usually fairly easy to tell who is bad because:

- They are foreign.
- They are ugly and have telltale features like scars.
- They look shifty and suspicious.
- They often engage in a few acts of random cruelty early on in the film to give us a clue.

Heroes and heroines, on the other hand, are generally good looking with a heart set on helping others, saving the situation or the world. Situations also come with a neat label – "world threat to be eradicated", "criminals planning a robbery", "murder to be solved". We are told, in no uncertain way, how to view situations and people. In real life there are no nicely predefined truths about others, their motives, or the various events that unfold around us. In real life the opportunity for personal interpretation of what happens is wide open.

Emotional experiences, then, are not just the reaction to events in our life – to what others say and do and to all the varied occurrences of life – but also to how we perceive and interpret these events. I don't mean that we consciously sit down and figure out what is happening to us – most of our interpretation, or "cognitive appraisal", is rapid, unconscious, and not always rational. Our tendency to appraise events in certain ways is influenced by our past experience and learning. Hopefully our spectacles are reasonably clear and we are seeing a good enough interpretation of the reality of what is happening. But our appraisal system can be skewed or distorted by early life experiences, so we continually misperceive the motives of others or misread events quite badly.

A last crucial feature of emotional experience is the unmistakably obvious point that emotions are felt. They are personally experienced by only one person: me. They represent "me" feeling the world around. Emotions are the central engine for experiencing "my world".[6] The things that happen to us, what people say and do, may be kind or cruel. A computer might be able to classify whether they are kind or cruel for us, by the use of clever algorithms, and that is that. They do not feel the impact of the cruelty or kindness. These events begin to be important to us, not because we classify them as important, like a computer, but because we feel them to be important. We personally experience the world through our emotional experience.

But there's another side to emotional experience. It doesn't exist in a vacuum. Emotions are exquisitely sensitive to thoughts and beliefs. Thoughts and emotions are usually so seamless it is difficult to know where one starts and the other ends. I would like to explore further the interconnection of emotions and beliefs.

Hidden Beliefs

In psychology our automatic beliefs about events – referred to as "cognitive appraisal" – how we mentally interpret situations – are generally accepted to be an integral part of what we feel and experience.[7, 8, 9] Aaron Beck, a psychiatrist with many years' experience treating depressed patients with psychoanalytical therapy, changed his approach to therapy in the 1970s by treating the hidden beliefs of the depressed patients about themselves, others, and the world in general.[10] He called these "hidden beliefs", "negative automatic thoughts", and this type of therapy, "Cognitive Therapy", concentrated very much on the here and now beliefs of depressed patients. Today this general approach has been used for numerous other psychological conditions, and Cognitive Therapy has become a worldwide phenomenon. Typical cognitive appraisals that patients might have are "I'm a failure" (an appraisal of oneself) or "they think I'm useless" (an appraisal of the other person's view of them), or "it will work out badly" (an appraisal of the future). The appraisal the person has about events going on around them will shape the emotions they experience, so negative pessimistic automatic beliefs will create miserable and sad emotional feelings. Changing the negative automatic thoughts to more realistic ones can lift the person's mood, which is the object of Cognitive Therapy. Depression is not the only emotional state this applies to. As explained in my self-help book on panic attacks,[11] appraisals of impending danger will produce feelings of fear. But this is all rather one-dimensional. Appraisal can be extremely complex, containing a mix of both positive and negative elements together. The emotions experienced can be as complex as the belief system underlying them – for instance, "I basically love this person but why did they say such a hurtful thing to me?" might engender feelings of hurt, betrayal, perplexity, anger, and hope in various combinations, which may change as the person talks it through and tries to understand what is going on.

How Do You Read the Trauma?

"Emotion schemas" is the name given by psychologists such as Jeffrey Young to a consistent pattern of bias in making appraisals. He pinpoints eleven "lifetraps", consistent ways of misperceiving others, which seriously distort a person's interpretation of events.[12] They include "abandonment" (expecting anyone you love to leave you); "mistrust" (expecting others to manipulate, lie, or take advantage of you); "unrelenting standards" (striving relentlessly to meet extremely high expectations of yourself and others); and "entitlement" (believing you are special and others exist to meet your needs). It should be pointed out that these are rather extreme patterns, which would make life a misery. Many people might have slight biases or "flavourings" of these negative schemas but predominately hold positive schemas.

In Post Traumatic Stress Disorder there are some very important things that are appraised. The trauma itself is usually so powerful and noxious that it can only be seen in a negative light. A beating, rape, or disfigurement almost carries its own automatic set of negative appraisals. Apart from this hugely negative core, subtleties in interpretation can surround a trauma.[13, 14] Here are some of the dimensions with illustrations of both "catastrophic" appraisals (on the left) and "realistic, positive" appraisals (on the right):

1. Danger/safety	
Everything is dangerous now.	It happened only once and is unlikely to happen again.
I thought the world was safe.	The world still can be safe.
2. Personality change	
I'll never be the same again.	Things always change.
My personality is shattered.	I'm still basically the same person.
3. Personal responsibility	
I could have done something to stop it.	I should not take too much personal responsibility.
It was my fault.	I was innocent.
4. Meaning	
Why me?	I wasn't personally singled out.
It's not fair.	It's life.
I must have done something wrong to deserve this.	It happens to saints and to sinners.

Making Sense of PTSD

Any significantly powerful event will almost force us to appraise it in some way. Post Traumatic Stress Disorder is such a powerful experience that in addition to appraising the trauma, the person will also appraise various elements of the disorder itself. Here are some important appraisals about the PTSD experience.

Again, catastrophic appraisals are on the left and realistic appraisals are on the right.

1. Appraisals about PTSD symptoms	
I'm going mad.	It's a curable condition.
This will last forever.	It is time limited.
2. Appraisals about traumatic memories	
If I let flashbacks happen I'll be overwhelmed.	If I let flashbacks happen ultimately their power will diminish.
Flashbacks will damage me.	Flashbacks are unpleasant but harmless.
I must keep flashbacks at bay.	I must allow memories to occur naturally.
3. Appraisals about reliving memories	
If I relive the memory the trauma will happen to me again.	Recalling memories cannot physically harm me.
If I relive a memory the anxiety will never stop.	The anxiety will subside.
Once I open up the traumatic memories I can never close the door.	Once I have faced the trauma it will start to subside.
4. Appraisals about experiencing emotions	
I don't want to think about the event.	I need to think about the event to work it through.
I cannot control the awful emotions.	I don't need to control anything – they will go of their own accord.
I cannot tolerate the emotions.	The emotions are unpleasant but safe.

5. Appraisals about expressing emotions	
If I talk about the trauma it will make it worse.	If I share the trauma it will be difficult but will assist my recovery.
It's dangerous to express emotions.	It's safe to express emotions.
If I cry I will lose control.	Crying is nature's healing process.
If I talk to others it will overwhelm, embarrass, or hurt them.	Other people want to help.
I do not want to involve others.	Other people can help me recover.
I need to keep my emotions tightly controlled.	I will get release by talking about my feelings.

These appraisals about facing unpleasant memories do not just result from the trauma itself but are also affected by the person's beliefs and views about emotions prior to the accident. In an Emotional Processing Group Therapy course that I set up with Primary Care counsellors Ann Henderson and Sandra May, for those who want to understand their emotions better, we spend one session trying to understand our "emotion rulebook". These are the subconscious rules that our family, culture, and early life experience instilled in us about how we should experience and express emotions.[15, 16, 17, 18, 19] In other words, it contains sets of emotion schemas. In the sessions we concentrate on tears, temper, and touch, but of course there are many other important emotions we have rules about. Our rulebook is usually hidden and we are unaware of it but nevertheless it exerts a strong influence on how we approach emotions. When a major trauma occurs in life it is likely that our existing rulebook will determine how we deal with the powerful emotions that are generated.

The Full Emotional Processing Model

In Chapter 6, the way in which a person stores and regulates memories was represented as a pictorial model showing all the relevant psychological processes. To complete the emotional processing model we need to add more than memory. We need to add the whole area of experiencing and expressing emotion – the complexity of which cannot really be captured in two boxes![20, 21, 22, 23, 24, 25] It shows how close the memory of the trauma and emotions are, and that emotion regulation is as much an attempt to control powerful emotions, as it is to control the memory as such.[26] The circle showing appraisal suggests how closely appraisal is linked with everything – appraisal of the trauma, of the memories, of memory recall, and of emotional experience. The large area preceding the trauma indicates the pervasive effect of emotion schemas, past memories, and previous traumas on the way in which the person reacts to a trauma.

Figure 2. Pictorial representation of Emotional Processing

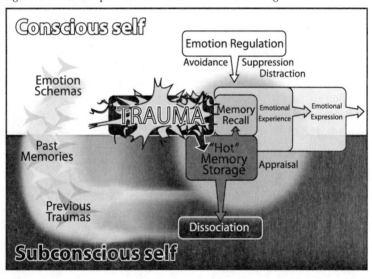

The Need for Therapy

Chapter 8

Susan's Story

The RAF Hercules was on a routine operational flight providing support to the Provincial Reconstruction Team (PRT) at Lashkar Gar (LKG), Afghanistan, at the time of the accident. The LKG Tactical Landing Zone (TLZ) is 6,800 ft long by 150 ft wide with a surface of compacted sand and gravel located on the south side of LKG town. The TLZ is used by UK forces and other agencies, including the UN and Red Cross.

The aircraft took off at 08:50 UTC (Coordinated Universal Time) from Kabul International Airport (KBL) to fly a routine logistics sortie to deliver cargo and personnel to LKG TLZ. After an uneventful medium level transit the aircraft landed at LKG at 10:20 UTC. Using a standard tactical landing technique the aircraft touched down some 500 ft from the runway threshold, reverse thrust was selected and the speed reduced without the need for wheel braking.

After 3 seconds, as the speed was nearing 70 knots, there was a loud bang from the port side of the aircraft in the vicinity of the port main landing gear, the force of which was felt throughout the aircraft. At the same time the flight deck crew saw tyre debris flying up in front of the aircraft and then became aware of structural damage to the No. 2 engine. The Captain ordered the Emergency Engine Shutdown Drill (EESD) on the No. 2 engine. He maintained directional control with nosewheel steering. Immediately after the shutdown of number 2 engine crew members observed a large amount of fuel leaking from the port wing area in the vicinity of the external tank pylon and that there was a fire in the vicinity of No. 1 engine. The Captain ordered the shutdown of the No. 1 engine

using the EESD. Whilst this drill was carried out crew members
observed that the fire was spreading across the whole wing. Realising
the severity of the situation the Captain brought the aircraft to
a halt near the northern end of the landing zone some 6,400 ft
from the touchdown point. He ordered the passengers and crew to
immediately carry out the Emergency Evacuation Drill.

Once all personal had evacuated the aircraft, the fire rapidly
destroyed the aircraft and cargo.

CONCLUSIONS: The Board concluded the XV206 was destroyed
after detonating an explosive device that was buried in the surface
of the LKG TLZ. After extensive investigation the Board concluded
that the device was an anti-tank landmine. This resulted in aircraft
debris puncturing the port wing fuel tanks, causing a major leak of
fuel that ignited, leading to an uncontrollable fire originating in the
port wing in the vicinity of the No. 1 engine.

Aviation Safety Network Report, 25 June 2006

Susan's Experience of the Crash

Susan, a British diplomat, was on board this flight in southern
Afghanistan in 2006. This is her account of what happened when
the Hercules hit the anti-tank mine and its effect on her in the
subsequent weeks and months.

I have a very clear, almost slow motion, memory of everything
that happened in the twenty seconds or so from hitting the anti-tank
mine (while the aircraft was still moving) to escaping the aircraft.
I was seated, like the rest of the passengers, with my back to the
fuselage. As we came in to land we had had the usual instruction to
"brace, brace, brace". We touched down. I heard the familiar roar of
the engines reversing their thrust, but then a few seconds later there
was a loud bang behind and to my right (towards the main landing
gear). Something hit me on the back of my head and I yelled "ouch"
(I think it was actually the side of the aircraft as it was blown in
with the blast). I later developed a large egg-type lump, but nothing
more serious. My first thought was that someone had thrown a rock
at the plane, but luckily for me, some other part of my brain had
recognized I might be in danger – I unlocked my seat belt and began
to look for my shoes (I had taken them off during the flight).

My neighbour asked me if I was OK, and I replied that I was fine.
Someone to my right called out for help. My helpful neighbour

went past me to get to him. I was still preoccupied with my head, trying to work out what had hit me, and finding my shoes (I never did find them). After a few seconds someone shouted "Fire Fire Fire!" followed quite quickly by "Out Out Out!" I looked to my right. I could see the silhouettes of people against an orange glow. The plane was on fire. I followed others to my left towards the front of the aircraft. We had to wait a few seconds longer until the aircraft had come to a stop. I remember this vividly as someone behind me, and closer to the fire, yelled at us to keep going, but there was nowhere to go. Once the aircraft stopped, I was about fourth or fifth to get out through the crew door. As I stood in the open doorway, I could feel the extreme heat coming from the blazing wing. It was so hot I couldn't look at it directly. I think this was the first point at which I fully and consciously realized the seriousness of the incident; and that I would not be going back to pick up my belongings once they had put the fire out.

I don't remember jumping the 5 feet from the doorway to the ground, but I am assured that I did. The soldiers that had escaped ahead of me were running in a straight line down the landing strip. That didn't feel right to me. I went with my instincts and ran diagonally away from the plane (to put it between me and any possible attackers). This also meant I was running towards the security team that had been waiting for our arrival. I couldn't believe how fast I was able to run, despite my bare feet and heavy body armour. I found it quite funny that I couldn't feel the sharp stones beneath my feet. One of the soldiers shouted at me to follow him. I followed until he wasn't looking then continued on my diagonal route. I got off the landing strip as soon as I could in case there were mines. (It was not until the accident investigation report was published about a year later that the cause of the explosion – an anti-tank mine – was confirmed.) Even at this early point I knew that it was nothing short of miraculous that I had escaped with my life. As a Christian, I believe God has a plan for my life. I was sure that I had been saved for a reason.

Once I reached the far edge of the strip, I stopped running – the security team were racing down the side of the landing strip towards me in their vehicles, and I didn't want to be run over. As I waited the few seconds it took them to reach me, I regained some feeling in my feet. I looked down and realized that I was standing on a thistle-like plant. Seconds later I was bundled into the back of one of the vehicles for protection. I sat in the rear foot well and pulled the thorns out of my feet while the team checked on the other survivors. The team-leader later told me that he had never been as relieved as when he looked into the back of the vehicle and saw me smiling back at him.

Thanks to the professionalism of the RAF crew, everybody escaped the aircraft with their lives. Two people that had been sitting immediately to my right, who had been closest to the explosion, did require some medical treatment, but both made full recoveries.

The Immediate Aftermath

That evening I had the opportunity to wind down with those who had been on the plane with me, including the crew to whom we owed our lives. This sharing of experiences, with a good dose of black humour thrown in, helped me to put my own experiences into context and build a better picture of what had happened. I was the only female on the flight, and try as I might, I could not get the others to understand the significance of having lost my hair straighteners!

The day after the crash everybody else who had been involved left for Kabul. I remained in southern Afghanistan, as this was where I worked. I went back to work two days after the incident, but it took a few weeks before I got completely back into my stride. It wasn't always easy trying to explain my feelings to work colleagues who had not shared my experience – I didn't want to be treated like a victim, but neither did I want to pretend nothing had happened. I worried that other than feeling more emotional than usual, I didn't really feel that there was anything wrong with me! I wrongly assumed that most people who had been in a near-death situation developed PTSD. I thought any sort of reaction was a sign of problems but that no symptoms might mean I was in denial.

The Foreign and Commonwealth Office (FCO) uses Trauma Risk Management (TRiM) to assess staff who have experienced a potentially traumatic incident. It is not a treatment or therapy, but does help identify those individuals who may need help to recover from a trauma or those who are more at risk of developing trauma-related illnesses such as PTSD. For me, the opportunity to talk through my experience with a trained assessor helped me to put events in order in my mind. It also helped me to address my misconceptions. This happened one week after the explosion. I learned that it was not unusual for people to experience some symptoms in the days and weeks following a traumatic event. These will normally disappear or improve with time – this is normal healing. The vast majority of those exposed to traumatic events recover on their own, without any need for external help. This reassured me that it was OK to feel OK.

I lost a lot of my belongings in the crash including most of my decent clothing. After a few days of walking round in my plastic flip flops, I decided I had to go up to the Embassy in Kabul to stock up on essentials. It was good to spend time with Embassy friends and colleagues. They understood enough about my life in the south to be good listeners. At this time, although I had talked to my family on the telephone about the crash, I didn't want to worry them by sharing all the details, and I didn't want to go back to the UK to see them until I felt I was back on my feet. The week-long break from the pace of work in the south also allowed me to sort out some of the personal administration created by the loss of my passport etc. Of all the things I had to deal with following the crash, it was the paperwork that drove me to distraction!

To get to Kabul I took my first flight since the mine-strike. I was apprehensive at the prospect. I chose a seat at the very back of the plane, as I knew that this was statistically the safest place. It also meant that I had a clear path to the nearest, and biggest, exit (the whole back end of a Hercules comes down to create a ramp). I was fine during the flight but had butterflies in my stomach as we came in to land. I held my breath as we touched down, and then slowly counted to ten as we braked. Nothing happened. I breathed a sigh of relief. As I walked off the back of the plane, I was a little shaky, but elated. One of the crew made a joke about me not having to worry as this plane was asbestos-lined. I realized that the crew had known that I had been involved in the crash, and had been looking out for me during the flight.

I continued to travel by Hercules aircraft during the last two months of my posting and it got easier with each subsequent flight. But I continued to be choosy about where I would sit on an aircraft for about a year, even after I had left Afghanistan. I preferred a seat towards the back of the plane, and was uncomfortable if there were any other passengers between me and my nearest escape route (I thought they might panic in the event of an accident and stop me getting off). On one occasion I cried (mainly in frustration) on the phone to British Airways when they refused to allow me to book an aisle seat in advance of travel without a note from my doctor. I wasn't sick. I didn't need help from my doctor. I was just a bit nervous about where I would sit. Surely this was understandable less than six months after a crash? Apparently not to British Airways. It is now three years since the crash, and I have no anxiety at all when flying – although I continue the tradition of counting to ten as we land!

The Personal Effect of the Trauma on Me

In the earliest days following the crash I felt quite emotionally bruised – able to take the big issues in my stride, but easily upset about small things. Memories and thoughts of the crash did not upset me, but I was reduced to tears on a couple of occasions by things I would normally have taken in my stride – for example, promised supplies from the Embassy not turning up. I found I was less tolerant, particularly of people I had found hard going before the incident. These feelings faded gradually, and after about four months I felt completely back to my pre-accident emotional self.

Loud or unexpected noises made me jump, and I discovered I no longer liked fireworks. An Embassy colleague explained that this was to be expected. He told me that the sound of a ship's bell still had an effect on him many years after he had been on a ship that sank. I was so grateful for that advice. It helped me to see my reaction as part of me and part of my history. Loud noises behind me sometimes still make me jump, but this has no impact on my day-to-day life. Fireworks do not bother me at all now.

In the first weeks and months following the crash, I sought out as much information as I could to help build my understanding of what had happened. I searched the Internet for newspaper articles and information on my incident and other Hercules accidents. I even found a military pilots' web forum where I could read their views on what had happened (they were all talking about it!).

I talked a lot to friends, family, and colleagues about the crash. This was key to my recovery. I have always been the type of person who articulates my thoughts and feelings in order to process them. Talking about the way I felt helped me immensely. To begin with I also felt that the crash was so central to who I was (or had become) that I had to tell people about it in order for them to understand me.

With time, the crash became less central in my own thoughts and how I defined myself. I no longer feel compelled to talk about my experience, but I still love to tell the story!

Immediately following the crash, the Foreign and Commonwealth Office (FCO) offered to curtail my posting and return me to the UK. I was grateful for the gesture, but was clear that I wanted to complete my posting. I wanted to remain with colleagues who had shared some of my experiences (if not the crash itself) while I recuperated, and I didn't want to feel beaten by whoever had attacked us. I only had just over two months left to serve anyway. I continued to be exposed to a level of danger on a daily basis. I did not become risk-averse; indeed if anything I became more determined to do my job despite the risks. I did find, however, that I was less willing to let others make decisions on my security for me. The desire to be in control of my environment continued after I left Afghanistan. I realized that my life had been saved by the actions of the RAF crew. I could not always count on the professionalism of others to get me out of a sticky situation. For about a year after the incident I would try to identify possible escape routes from buildings in case of fire (or attack while still in Afghanistan). The first thing I bought and installed in my new London flat was a smoke detector. On the second anniversary of the July 2005 London bombings, and just over a year after my incident, I took a backpack to work containing everything I would need to make my own way home should there be another attack, including trainers in case I had to do the 4-mile journey by foot.

Survivorship

I feel that overall my experience has had a positive effect on me. I know that I responded well under pressure and I know that I can trust my instincts. Surviving the crash (and the rest of my posting in Afghanistan) has made me stronger, more accepting of my own failures, and has given me a better sense of perspective. I used to worry about my own mortality. Now I find that while I am more appreciative of life in general, I have no fear of it ending. I spend much less time worrying about everyday things. I remember on one occasion not long after I returned to the UK, I stood my ground on an issue with a very senior colleague. He accepted my point of view and we resolved the issue we had been discussing. It was only after

I was back at my desk that I realized the change in me – had that situation happened to me before, I would have fretted about how to approach my colleague, and if I had gathered the courage to do so, I would have been shaking in my boots afterwards. In that situation, and in others since, I have applied a simple rule to how much time I should spend worrying over something – will someone die if I get this wrong? I took the job in Afghanistan because I believed that it was God's plan for me. It wasn't an easy decision – I felt that he was asking me to be willing to give up my life to follow his will – but I reached the conclusion that it would be far better to die young and in God's will, than to reach a ripe old age but live outside his plan for me. Because of what God had asked of me, I had expected to die in Afghanistan. From the moment I stood with the burning plane behind me, I was aware of the significance of what had just happened. He asked me to be willing to die – and he showed me how easily I could have – but then he saved me. Since that point, I have looked to the future with a sense of excitement and purpose; I know God has further plans for me.

It is very important to me that I am able to use my own experiences to help and support others who experience trauma. I am now a trained Trauma Risk Management assessor and have participated on two FCO deployments to support staff involved in violent terrorist incidents overseas.

Chapter 9

Healthy and Unhealthy Reactions to Trauma

Susan must have been doing something right. Being trapped in a burning plane is a serious, life-threatening trauma, yet she did not develop Post Traumatic Stress Disorder. Was she a strong person? Was she naturally fearless? Did she have genetic strength that prevented her from developing PTSD?

If we look beyond the trauma to the way Susan dealt with it, we see a catalogue of good practice. Susan, whether by accident or design, did everything to assist her own recovery. Here is a list of all the positive features:

1. Susan felt that the first night was really important to her recovery. All the service personnel involved in the crash – soldiers, aircrew, and civilians like Susan, met up and drank the night away. I'm not advocating alcohol as the solution, but rather all the survivors were together in a cohesive group, endlessly going over the story of what happened as if collectively they were trying to make sense of the experience. As Susan said, there was a lot of black humour, but collectively it was as if the group were mastering the trauma. Their words and communal spirit contained and controlled the memory, casting it in a particular light while making this a shared experience, not the fate of an isolated individual.

2. Prior to, during, and after the explosion Susan was part of an excellent support system. She was part of a unit whose aircrew and soldiers were highly professional and knew what they were doing. There was a feeling of professionalism and support not

just from the military but also from a security team that was waiting for them and later from her work colleagues.

3. Susan allowed herself to think about the trauma and talk to others. She talked about her experiences with her family, friends, other crash victims, and Embassy colleagues. This probably served a twofold function of expressing her feelings and helping her to mentally put events in order.

4. Susan cried – it did not seem to be direct tears about the trauma but more from minor irritations. It would perhaps have been more cathartic for her to cry about the trauma, but anyway she did cry, which is an important form of release.

5. She actively sought out as much information as she could to put the pieces of the experience together, including the military pilot's web forum, where the pilots were also trying to understand what had happened.

6. She did not immediately retreat from the situation, but worked for a few days, followed by a holiday.

7. She had the opportunity, a week after the explosion, to talk to a Trauma Risk Management staff member, where the expert advice helped to correct certain misconceptions about PTSD, as well as going over the trauma once again.

8. She had prior knowledge about PTSD, so apart from being concerned about not feeling enough symptoms, she was not caught out by perplexing symptoms.

9. After a short interval she got back into an aircraft again, at first into a Hercules aircraft, the same as in the crash, but in other aircraft later. Although she was particular about where she sat and she had her own "countdown" ritual on landing, she allowed herself to be exposed to many of the original "evoking stimuli" until they no longer evoked powerful emotions.

10. She had a wider philosophical perspective on what had happened. She believed that God had a plan for her and although traumatic, this was part of that plan. Much of the perplexity around "Why me?", "It's not fair", was offset by this greater, more positive perspective.

11. Prior to the accident, Susan had a fairly good understanding of who she was, her own emotions, and although quite a rational person was able to value, tune in to, and listen to her own emotions. Consequently after the accident she did not ignore her emotional life.

One way or another, whether by luck, design, or a combination of both, Susan was a textbook case of what to do right. Her story was not picked for this reason; she just happened to be a close friend who had recently survived a significant trauma as I was writing this book.

What Do You Bring to the Trauma?

Psychiatrists J. Tichener and W. Ross, writing in 1974,[1] used an interesting analogy of a flood to illustrate how different people react to a trauma. When the flood waters cover the earth there is no way of telling what lies beneath. When the waters recede sometimes the landscape looks much as it did before the flood, but at other times there have been massive changes, with long-lasting damage. Likewise, when the initial effects of the trauma subside, one person may be left unscathed and another traumatized. Although this analogy nicely illustrates how difficult it is to predict who will get PTSD and who won't, to my mind it suggests the impact is rather random. I would suggest that we can understand more about who is vulnerable and who is less so by looking at the emotional processing styles that they bring to the trauma.

During childhood, adolescence, and adulthood everyone develops strategies and approaches for coping with problems in their lives. So when trauma strikes in adult life, they will face it with a pre-existing style of emotional coping. As a child they may have learned to bring their worries to their parents, teachers, or close friends to talk through. Alternatively, they might have developed a more self-sufficient approach, such as trying to face and understand things themselves. On the other hand, they may have developed dysfunctional emotional coping styles, which may seem sensible at the time but don't really remove emotional pain in the long term. This could include self-harm, suicide attempts, drugs, and alcohol to anaesthetize the pain. Returning to the traumatic event in adulthood there will be many well-worn thoughts, strategies, and reactions already in waiting. PTSD is not just a random effect of the "floodwaters of the trauma", but also depends on all those personal reactions and styles of emotional coping that have been previously developed.

Those First Crucial Hours

Mostly in this book I have concentrated on people who have developed Post Traumatic Stress Disorder. This is a long-term reaction – by definition, PTSD cannot be diagnosed until one month after the trauma. What about those crucial first hours, days, and weeks? What is normal? What is a healthy and what is an unhealthy reaction?

There have been many studies interviewing trauma victims soon after the incident, and following them up to see whether problems persist or, as with Susan, fade into the background. There have been studies of fire-fighters exposed to a major fire disaster in the Australian bush,[2] of military personnel from the Vietnam war,[3] terrorist bombings,[4] civilians caught in the first Gulf War,[5] motor accident victims,[6] and train drivers involved in railway accidents.[7] They all suggest that a range of distressing reactions is very common. Shock, disbelief, "being in a daze", numbness, confusion, disorientation, and dreamlike states are often the first reactions after surviving a trauma. In the next few days, survivors may feel anxious or over aroused, with difficulty sleeping, irritability, poor concentration, restlessness, agitation, or depression. A group of psychologists who studied the psychological impact of the first Gulf War on Israeli citizens found such high rates of distress in 80 per cent of their sample that they concluded, "the acute stress reaction constellation is almost universal"[8, 9]. Although PTSD refers to a longer-term reaction, many psychologists note that Post Traumatic Stress-type symptoms are extremely common in the first few days after a trauma. Psychiatrist Arich Shaler, studying injured survivors of a terrorist attack, found that intrusive memories of the trauma appeared in the majority of survivors within forty-eight hours of the attack. He noted that some survivors found the repeated memories intolerable, while others were less distressed by them. His clinical observations suggested an active processing phase where "many survivors are judging themselves and re-evaluating their actions (or their failure to act) with particular intensity during that period". In study after study intrusive memories tend to be the symptom experienced most frequently, almost an integral part of a normal reaction to trauma. Intrusive memories themselves do not predict the later development of full-blown PTSD. After an intensive period of mentally working through the trauma the intrusive memories seem to fade in many people. The presence of intrusive memories in the early stages isn't predictive. It seems to be the intrusive memories along with the attempt to avoid the memories that predict PTSD more accurately.[10, 11] The crucial factor, then, seems to be trying to avoid intrusive memories, not having the memories as such.

In the 1980s, many private psychology firms were set up to provide "trauma de-briefing" for those who had just experienced a major disaster or trauma. Teams of counsellors quickly sped to the scene of a major disaster to help the survivors talk over the trauma. "Psychological de-briefing is a waste of time," concluded Simon Wessely, on the basis of a systematic review of well-controlled research studies into immediate trauma de-briefing in 2000.[12] At best it was ineffective and at worst it was counter-productive, generating more Post Traumatic Stress reaction than reducing it.[13]

It is now realized that timing is the important element. At first, during the shock phase, the person needs to be left alone to calm down and let the memories of the trauma consolidate. Over the successive hours and days the person usually incessantly mentally replays the scene in an attempt to understand and emotionally process what has happened to them. Usually, the greater the trauma is, the more emotional turmoil that will be generated. The trauma will be foremost in the person's mind as they try to make sense of the experience. If the person typically has learned to handle distress by suppressing their feelings, or avoiding unpleasant reminders of the distress, they may bring that to their first hours after the trauma. They may try not to think of what has happened, to block it off, or suppress feelings. Because the trauma is so powerful, attempts at stemming the tide are pretty ineffective.

The psychologist D. Wegner introduced the term "the ironic process" in 1998 to refer to a sort of rebound effect when we try to control thoughts.[14, 15] In his famous "white bear" experiments his research subjects were told they must not think about white bears or the phrase "white bear" for two minutes. They were allowed to think about anything else but not white bears. When the two minutes started, what happened? They couldn't get white bears out of their mind. Attempts to not think of white bears had the reverse effect.

If a person becomes afraid of intrusive memories, it provides strong motivation to try to suppress them in some way. They may try to avoid reminders of the trauma or those little triggers that so easily set off flashbacks, or try to suppress the flashback once it starts. The ironic process that Wegner described will ensure that they become engaged in a pitched battle with the thoughts that just will not disappear.

The pre-existing emotional strategies that the person brings to the trauma can contribute towards the development of Post Traumatic Stress Disorder. Someone who does not understand or dislikes their emotions or who typically avoids or suppresses negative emotional experiences will be more prone to develop PTSD than someone with a more accepting approach to emotions. But this is not the whole picture. Emotional processing style is one factor among others that increases proneness to PTSD. Some of the other factors are: severity of the trauma, the existence of previous traumas, and the lack of a social support network.

Guidelines for Reacting to a Trauma

There is a time for everything
and a season for every activity under heaven
… a time to weep and a time to laugh
a time to mourn and a time to dance
… a time to tear and a time to mend
a time to be silent and a time to speak
Ecclesiastes 3:1, 4, 7

What to do in the first hours and days after experiencing a traumatic event differs from what to do if Post Traumatic Stress symptoms set in and become rather permanent. Anything up to one month is not regarded as Post Traumatic Stress, and although symptoms may be unusual, powerful and distressing they are normal in the first few weeks.

The essential first step is to get out of the danger zone, find a place of security, get assistance, and be treated for all medical and physical problems. At this stage you might be in a daze, not thinking much at all – that's OK. Practical physical help is crucial at this stage, not psychological assistance.

Next, get home or to a place of safety, security, and quiet. Rest a lot, sleep, eat, drink alcohol (in moderation) if desired. If it's appropriate, do as Susan did and talk with other survivors, but this isn't always possible. After a while the sense of being in a daze may be replaced with going over and over the trauma in one's mind. This might be in the form of flashbacks that keep intruding into the mind, or more of a conscious decision and desire to go over it again and again. This should not be blocked but allowed to just happen. It's safe enough. Feelings of being in turmoil, distressed, and agitated are to be expected – that's normal.

Third, if it feels right, start talking to others, such as friends and family, about what happened – this will probably involve repeating it several times in the process of grappling with the events, but that's all right – finding a sympathetic ear is important. Writing down the experience is helpful too. There is no obligation to talk about it – whatever comes naturally. You should not be pressed into talking until you are ready, but if you haven't spoken about it by the second week, then it's probably time to push through the barrier and get talking.

In the first few days after the trauma, rest. It's probably best not to get back into the flow of things, or go back to work. If work is unavoidable, it should be kept absolutely minimal. Work colleagues may be quite understanding about this and not expect full attendance too quickly. You should not feel pressured to return to the same level of work as before. It's not weak to stay out of things or take it easy. After a serious trauma no one can expect instant recovery.

Cry, cry, cry. Crying is nature's healing process and it's perfectly normal and healthy to cry, for men as well as women.[16] Some people prefer to cry alone. Sometimes the reaction of others is helpful, sometimes unhelpful, so choosing who to cry with or talk to can be important. You should get as much support around you as possible.

It will be natural over days and weeks to try to figure out exactly what happened – it's good to try to put it together as much as possible in one's mind, but again there should not be any pressure to do this. At this stage there's no need to seek professional psychological help. Don't be thrown by Post Traumatic type symptoms in the first month – nightmares, flashbacks, disorientation, feelings of unreality, agitation and poor concentration. They are normal and should pass after resting and working things through sufficiently. It's a matter of timing – let the mind get on with the natural work of processing the trauma at its own pace. If the symptoms are as powerful as ever after the one-month point, then it is time to seek help. A visit to one's General Medical Practitioner would be a good starting point.

Chapter 10

Emotional Processing Therapy

Long-term symptoms of Post Traumatic Stress are an indication that the emotional power of the memory of the trauma is still intact. "Long-term" refers to anything over one month, but many PTSD sufferers have experienced symptoms for much longer than this, even years. The symptoms are rather like smoke from an emotional fire still smouldering. The symptoms indicate that the trauma has not yet been emotionally processed. When the emotional memory has been successfully processed, the symptoms of PTSD will subside, including nightmares, flashbacks, hyperarousal, irritability, and numbed feelings, regardless of how long PTSD has lasted. The *Diagnostic and Statistical Manual* regards attempts to avoid reminders of the traumatic memory as a symptom of PTSD. I would suggest that they are not a symptom at all, but a coping mechanism that holds the key to whether other PTSD symptoms diminish or increase.

Section IV of this book describes in detail a self-help programme for people who might have developed the long-term symptoms of Post Traumatic Stress Disorder. What follows now is an overview of the psychological stages that are necessary to achieve successful emotional processing. It presents the broad ideas behind Emotional Processing Therapy, but for more detailed practical help, Section IV is the place to go.

1. Access the traumatic memories. First, for successful emotional processing, the memory must be allowed to enter consciousness, not just for a few seconds like a flashback that might be suppressed, but long enough to be felt and explored.[1] This involves engaging all the sensory elements of the memory, such as sights, sounds, smells, or kinaesthetic sensations. There may be many elements of the memory to be explored and understood, such as exactly what happened, in what sequence, and what was most distressing. Sometimes this brings new understandings that themselves need further exploration, such as anger towards the perpetrator. The total memory does not need to be recalled in one sitting – this may be a very long process.

2. Experience emotions – even the negative ones. It is surprising how many people don't like emotions. Some don't like anything that moves emotionally speaking and would be happy to remain at a sort of anaesthetic level. Some wish to eradicate those distressing and disturbing emotions that eat away at them, but perhaps retain their pleasant emotions. In PTSD it is understandable how people would want to remove the terrible distress, fear, panic, anger, confusion, and unbearable arousal that is associated with the trauma. But removing those distressing emotions is the wrong solution. The emotions are there for a good reason. They tell us something is wrong. Something needs to be sorted out. The emotional turmoil of the trauma has not yet been healed.[2, 3, 4] When the cause of the distressed emotions has been dealt with, the emotions will subside to a manageable level, as a river in torrent can settle to a calm flow once the snows in the mountains and hills have thawed. It is possible for all the emotional turmoil that constitutes PTSD to subside, but a direct assault on the emotions themselves is not the solution. Healing the memory of the trauma is the solution.[5] Having the capacity to feel enjoyment, happiness, love, contentment, success, or just the mild daily pleasures of being alive inevitably includes the capacity for feeling hurt too. If we could pick and choose our emotions to include all the joys and exclude the sorrows, life would soon become topsy-turvy. Instead of being upset when a loved one leaves for a long journey, we'd be as happy as when they first came home. If they died, there would be joy and no grief.

So the powerful emotional experiences that accompany the memory should be allowed to be experienced and lived with, although extremely distressing. A common mistaken "emotional belief" is that "if I remember it, it will happen all over again". Although this is illogical, when put like this, it is a powerful unconscious idea that lies beneath the surface. If the person allows themself to experience the distress associated with the memories, they discover from personal experience that the accident does not repeat itself. The essential element here is "discovering from personal experience". It is not an intellectual change of ideas, but an experiential change. This disconfirmation in experience helps them to make real progress.

3. Express emotions. Emotional feelings need to be expressed both to bring relief and to allow further exploration of the memory. Tears are a direct expression of hurt, which often bring a sense of release as suggested in the phrase "having a good cry". Tears can also act as a signpost to us, directing our attention towards things that are significant, even though we have not mentally worked out the connection. For instance, if a person always cries at a particular part of the memory recall, say the reaction of the paramedic to them, this indicates that there is something especially significant about the encounter. It needs to be explored further to increase understanding.[6, 7]

Although talking is not a direct expression of pain like crying, it is a kind of expression that allows more exploration of the hurt and ultimately a better understanding of it.[8] Words are a major vehicle for our expression of feelings. We can share with others and explain what we are feeling. Words give access to the inner world of feeling, and quite complex emotional ideas can be expressed. The whole field of psychotherapy is predicated on the use of words to unlock and express inner disturbance. Sometimes words are accompanied by emotion, as when psychotherapy touches on a sensitive area and the patient begins to cry. The act of explaining one's feelings in words may be a cathartic release of feelings but also expresses in detail aspects of emotional experience previously hidden.[9] And this identification of feelings often leads on to examining the root causes of the distressed feelings.

Writing down words in the form of a diary or record has similarities with sharing with a close friend or psychotherapist, but of course in written, not verbal form. The diary may be written to oneself, or to imagined others. How it differs from live conversation is that there is no other person to provide feedback, support, or insights. It makes writing a more personal exploration of feeling rather than a medium for change. Ever since Anna "O", Freud's first psychotherapy patient,[10] who described her "talking therapy" or "chimney sweeping", psychotherapy in its various forms and guises has had a major influence on Western culture. Throughout history, talking with family and friends, or confiding to a close friend or a priest has played a similar role, but without the formal professional psychotherapy setting. I don't want to suggest that human beings were deficient in emotional expression before the advent of psychotherapy – obviously they coped pretty well for thousands of years.

There are subtler but less direct types of expression found in the arts, such as expression via music, dance, painting, sculpture, movement, and mime. A significant proportion of our culture is taken up with the myriad expressions of the finer and more expressive aspects of the human spirit. Those artists and musicians who convey some deeper sense of emotions through their art are often the most successful. My wife and I were lucky enough to get front row seats to a monthly series of concerts featuring world-class virtuosi. Not only were they masters of their instruments, but from close up the intensity of their absorption in the music shown by their faces and bodies spoke of a deep emotional experience.

The Essential Ingredients of Therapy

The therapy is called Emotional Processing Therapy because it emphasizes the central role of both the unprocessed emotional memory of the trauma and the type of emotional processing style used by the person. The central aim of therapy is to reduce the emotional power of the traumatic memory, but in order to do this the emotional processing style of the person needs to be addressed too.

How does the therapy work? This may not be a question that bothers a lot of people. "If it works, it works; that's good enough for me." Psychologists, however, are obsessed with this question. It is essential for us to know by what mechanisms a therapy works; there are multitudes of psychology journal articles written on this, much academic debate, and different schools of interpretation. Just so that you don't think we are simply obsessional, full stop, there is a reason for this attempt to pin down psychological "mechanisms". Understanding the psychological principles behind why people improve in therapy enables us to be much more accurate in the way in which therapy is carried out and can produce new and better techniques.

The systematic facing of traumatic memories has been shown in numerous clinical trials and in scientific reviews to be the most effective treatment of PTSD to date. It is recommended as the treatment of choice by the National Institute of Clinical Effectiveness

(NICE), the scientific evaluation arm of the NHS.[11] "Exposure Based Therapy", "Prolonged Exposure" and "Trauma Focused Therapy" are all different terms for therapies in which facing the traumatic memory is central. They are all encompassed under the very broad umbrella term "Cognitive Behaviour Therapy" (CBT). In letters to solicitors and court reports about PTSD I avoid using the term CBT because it is a broad term that could refer to several different approaches, often quite different. It is just not specific enough.

Emotional Processing Therapy uses everything in Prolonged Exposure or Exposure Based Therapy, but it has more.[12, 13] The extra dimension in Emotional Processing Therapy is the far greater emphasis on the emotional aspects of therapy. The person's pre-existing emotion schemas, or "emotion rulebook", are crucial in understanding how PTSD develops, and for therapy to be most successful their emotional processing style needs to be included. Not only that, but a central mechanism for understanding why the therapy is so successful is the change in emotional processing style that it evokes.

In any psychological therapy there are sets of interlocking processes at work that produce the beneficial therapeutic effect, not just one process, and it's the same for Emotional Processing Therapy. I would suggest that these are the essential psychological ingredients:

1. The initial change in the person's emotional processing style to a more accepting, open style allows them to start the therapy, persist in it to the degree that is required, and continue it outside the therapy office and after therapy is over. Particularly for a self-help approach, one needs to be firmly convinced of the importance of facing emotional memories rather than avoiding or suppressing them.

2. The next stage is for the person to access the powerfully distressing emotional memories of the trauma.[14, 15] They need to face many of the trigger stimuli that they have previously avoided, including allowing themselves to visualize the experience, think thoughts about it, say words like "crash" or "screaming in agony" – feeling the bodily sensations or sounds experienced in the trauma. In short, they need to face all the trigger stimuli associated with the trauma. Unless the memories are accessed no change is possible.

3. The person needs to allow themselves to face the trigger stimuli and the emotions they evoke long enough for the emotional reaction to fade. How does it fade? This process is often referred to as habituation – an emotional feeling cannot be felt indefinitely unless there is something to stir it up.[16, 17, 18] Emotions are naturally quite fleeting, and it is rare for someone to stare persistently at the evoking stimuli, especially if it is noxious. This is a natural physiological fading process. This works similarly for positive emotions as well as negative ones. See what happens if you try to hold on to joy – it will evaporate before your eyes in the same way that fear will. It simply loses its power to evoke emotion.[19]

4. This natural process of fading has enormous therapeutic repercussions:

- It can invalidate appraisals about PTSD symptoms and traumatic memories, e.g., "it will last forever", "flashbacks will make me mentally disintegrate".
- It can invalidate appraisals about the trauma, e.g. "everything is dangerous now".
- It can change emotion schemas, e.g. "I must always avoid powerful emotions."[20, 21, 22, 23]

This last point suggests a much more fundamental change in how emotions are handled. The person may have learned to avoid exploring distressing emotions simply because this was the style they absorbed in their family from an early age. In this sense the therapy may be changing a fixed emotional habit. It might be even more significant if the avoidance cloaked early abuse; for instance, a child may have learned to shut down and be quiet when father returns home, to avoid being hit. For this person, facing the memory of their recent trauma of, say, a car accident, may help move them towards a much more open approach to feeling emotions.

5. Traumatic memories are stored in terms of sense impressions, with intense emotional associations, without logic, without words, without a narrative structure, and without a properly unfolding time sequence or "time tags". In other words they are stored in a fragmentary way without context and with minimal organization. Talking about the memory puts a far greater structure and organization upon it.[24, 25]

6. After talking about it the memory is re-stored in a more organized, verbally accessible manner.

7. Allowing oneself to feel emotions previously hidden, to cry and talk about the trauma, is a release similar to Freud's notion of catharsis. One could say in reliving there is release.[26, 27, 28, 29]

8. Talking about traumatic memories allows the person to understand, piece together, "put in place", what happened. This may be assisted by newspaper reports, police accounts, witness reports, etc. Not only does talking help to put together events but also to understand one's own emotional reactions more, such as guilt or anger, which hitherto were unidentified. The analogy I often use with patients is that at first the memory is like a jigsaw puzzle with the pieces all mixed up. As the trauma is discussed, they put more and more pieces together until the final picture makes sense. It is usually the case that as they put together pieces of their own jigsaw of events, that they feel a much greater sense of completeness and control.[30]

I have described eight processes underlying effective therapy, encompassing physiological habituation, change in cognitive and emotional belief structure, reorganization of memories, emotional expression, and increasing understanding. All of these can be effectively described under one heading. It could all be referred to as "emotional processing".

Self-Help Programme for PTSD

Chapter 11

Max's Story

Max arrived thirty minutes before the session was due to begin. He parked his car in the quiet road outside the therapy office and sat there. His body was telling him "Why not give it a miss – drive back home", but he knew he had to get help for his problems. He was trying to pluck up enough courage to open the door and walk up the drive for his first appointment with Professor Roger Baker, Consultant Clinical Psychologist, as it said on the letterhead. Finally he took the plunge, walked up the drive, and pressed the doorbell. So began our first session together.

Max had been referred to me by solicitors Knighton-Royal following an accident at work for which he was suing his employers. This was a first interview session to assess whether he was suffering from Post Traumatic Stress Disorder and if so what advice I would give about possible treatment options.

Max was a quiet, unassuming man, whose strong desire to get help for his problems had overcome his reluctance to talk. After I had shown him to the therapy room and we had both settled down with a cup of tea (an essential therapeutic ingredient in England), I asked him in the most general of ways to tell me how his accident had affected him. I knew from the solicitors that his fall from a rooftop at work was the focal accident, but to ask about the accident itself at this point would be demanding too much. It is much easier for sufferers to talk about the impact of the accident on their life, because that is one stage removed from the traumatic emotional memories. So that is where we began.

He started off by telling me he had sustained a serious injury to his hand, for which he required three lots of surgery, with pins put in the wrist. He had "badly crushed nerves, which give him pins and needles". He said he had been sleeping very poorly and having nightmares – he would wake up with the pillow soaking wet. His partner told him that during sleep he grabbed her as if he were falling. The accident had happened thirteen months previously; the combination of his hand injury, surgery, and his psychological state meant he had not worked in this period and was finding it a financial strain to support his partner and two children.

"The worst bit about the nightmares," he continued, "is waking up with a falling sensation and remembering the noise as I hit the concrete." He was also concerned about the way he treated his children. "If the children are playing and they slam a door, it frightens me. I jump out of my skin. I'm always telling them off. If we're watching a DVD in the evening I get so agitated if the children talk in the middle of it that I stand up and switch it off. It's not fair on them."

I continued to ask him how the accident had affected him, checking whether he spontaneously revealed any other Post Traumatic Stress symptoms. Already he had indicated that nightmares, increased startle response, and irritability – cardinal symptoms of PTSD – were troubling him. He did report thinking about the accident every day, and that it "popped into my mind". When I mentioned the word "flashbacks", he immediately understood what I meant. He said they came about four times a day. He also mentioned problems seeing heights on the TV and told me, "If I stand at the top of the stairs it brings it back – nerves."

At this point when he was more relaxed and we had established a degree of rapport together, I asked him to tell me briefly about the accident. He did not describe much about what happened, but said more about some of the thoughts and sensations after the fall. "For a split second I couldn't hear. I was in so much pain. I was sick, sweating, with a buzzing in my ears. I remember thinking, 'What's going on?' My middle finger was standing up. I couldn't move, and thought 'My back, I hope I haven't broken it'. I was in so much pain, confused and paralysed."

I asked what he thought would happen to him. He replied, "When I was falling, for a split second I thought I would probably die. I thought after the accident I would be paralysed." An ambulance arrived and the paramedics gave him morphine for the pain. "They said I was lucky – it could have been my back, head, or neck."

Next I tried to discover to what degree he tried to avoid memories of the accident. He seemed to be avoiding quite a lot in his life, such as reminders of the accident on the TV; he could not go back to the area in which the accident happened; at first he could not speak to his workmates; and he stopped his regular games of snooker – initially because of his hand injury, but later "because I didn't want to go out". He added, "My partner talks to me, she's great. I talk a bit, but don't like to. She says it will help."

As part of a standard assessment for PTSD I ask the person to fill in a number of standardized psychometric questionnaires covering psychological symptoms, self-esteem, quality of life, response to trauma, and emotional processing style. Actually, at this stage in the interview I had no doubt that Max was suffering from Post Traumatic Stress Disorder. He had described three symptoms in the category of "persistently experiencing the traumatic event" (one is required for a *DSM-IV* diagnosis), five symptoms in the category of "avoidance of stimuli associated with the trauma and numbing of general responsiveness" (three are required for a diagnosis), and four symptoms in the category of "increased arousal" (two are required for a diagnosis). Together, these symptoms fulfilled the *DSM-IV* diagnosis for Post Traumatic Stress Disorder. For the solicitors report and for any subsequent legal enquiries I was professionally obliged to go for "overkill" and ask him to plough through the battery of standardized psychological assessments.

As I sat there in the evening light waiting for him to complete the questionnaires, I was already mentally writing the letter to the solicitor, Miles Nash, whom I knew quite well. I would report on Max's problem of PTSD symptoms, his psychometric assessment scores, and how his life had been affected by the trauma. I would suggest that the problems could persist for many months, even years, without help, and recommend a course of psychological therapy based on Trauma Exposure techniques "delivered by a Clinical Psychologist working for the UK National Health Service or a Chartered Clinical Psychologist of the British Psychological Society".

I liked Max. He was unassuming and genuine and I think underplayed the degree of his suffering. I hoped he might be sent back to me for therapy, but had to leave that decision to the solicitor. Sometimes, for legal reasons, solicitors like to separate the psychologist who conducted the assessment from the therapist. Over the years I have come to specify "Clinical Psychologist" as the appropriate therapist, because counsellors and general psychotherapists, although excellent in many ways, may lack the specific Cognitive Behavioural skills for PTSD. Conversely, recommending "Cognitive Behaviour Therapy", an umbrella term for many different therapies, is too broad. "Trauma Exposure", or "exposure to the traumatic memories", specifies what type of Cognitive Behaviour Therapy approach is appropriate.

"Is an intrusive thought the same as a flashback?" asked Max, jolting me from my reverie. He had got stuck on one of the questionnaire items.

"Oh, pretty much the same, except flashbacks are often a very visual type of intrusive thought... but yes, it's getting at the same thing."

Max finished the assessments quite quickly, although I could see he was having problems, holding the pen with his right hand, and sometimes using his left hand to adjust and steady the pen. After quickly scoring the main assessment results, I explained to Max what the interview and test results showed, what the typical symptoms of PTSD were, and that this is a normal response to an abnormal event. It occurred quite frequently, I said, giving a little bit of history about PTSD identified in solders in the First World War. I emphasized it was not a mental illness but a psychological reaction to trauma. He showed all the classic symptoms of PTSD, but of course the trauma in his case was not war, but falling from the roof. He seemed satisfied with this.

Next I told him what I would put into the letter to his solicitors, recommending a course of Trauma Exposure by a qualified Clinical Psychologist. "Would that be you?" he asked, a bit anxiously.

"I can't say at this stage, but I hope so."

He then told me the story of him sitting in his car for half an hour plucking up the courage to come in, and that now he'd got to know me he hoped it would be me and not someone new.

Before we finally finished, I felt it was really important to explain what "Trauma Exposure" might involve, because it is somewhat counter-intuitive to a PTSD sufferer and requires a bit of mental adjustment to contemplate. Usually I spend time explaining the nature of therapy in the first therapeutic session but some pre-therapy explanation could be helpful for Max, I thought.

"Although in part you've told me about the accident," I said, "you've not really gone back there yet, have you?"

"I told my solicitor all the facts."

"Could you say you have really re-visited what happened?"

"I had to keep myself in check when I told him..."

"In check?"

"Yes, all my life I've not been able to share emotionally, so I just told him the bare bones from... like a bit of a distance."

"One of the problems in Post Traumatic Stress Disorder is that the memory of the trauma is still raw and emotionally powerful. The person doesn't want to think about the trauma because it's too painful. But that's the problem. Because they're always avoiding visiting the trauma it doesn't have a chance to lose its powerful emotional grip. Trauma Exposure involves helping the person recall the traumatic event in detail. This needs quite a lot of emotional preparation – so as psychologists we wouldn't jump straight into re-visiting the trauma. It has to be when the person is ready – in their own time. It's a difficult time that can go on for weeks, until the person fully processes the emotional memory of the trauma. When it has lost its emotional power, the symptoms of PTSD tend to subside."

"Like having the calm after the storm."

"Yes, that's right."

I hadn't been sure until this point that he was following me so well.

"The research evidence is that this is the most effective treatment for PTSD, but it's hard to go through, and not right for everybody. What do you think?"

"It sounds scary. My hands were sweaty as you described it. But if I thought about it and plucked up the courage, I'd be ready to give it a try."

"Like you plucked up the courage to come into my office a couple of hours ago?"

"Yes, I suppose so."

As further preparation to help Max "think about the therapy", I recommended my book on emotional processing, which generally explains the importance of facing, not avoiding, emotions. He took all the details with him and seemed keen to make a start.

Over the next weeks I finished the assessment report on Max for Knighton-Royal solicitors, fleshing out the details to the imaginary report I had planned during our session. A short time later Miles Nash contacted me and asked me to go ahead with treatment as suggested. I didn't know until later that Max had had a hand in this decision.

The Return of Max

I had originally planned to write this chapter about what therapy involved by going through the programme stage by stage. I will still do this in the following chapters, but I thought a well-worked example of what goes on in Emotional Processing Therapy would be the best starting point. I picked Max as a good, straightforward example of the therapy. He was very happy for me to use his case in the book and to quote him verbatim if appropriate. So having introduced you to Max, and given you a glimpse of what therapy might involve, I would like to go through his therapy programme step by step.

Our first three sessions were in January and early February 2008. The sessions were held in my therapy office in the early evening and lasted about one hour. While I'm sure that these sessions were therapeutic in many ways, their main purpose was to prepare Max for the apex of the therapy – facing those memories he had been trying so hard to avoid. As promised in our first assessment session, I would not start "exposure to the traumatic memories" until Max was ready. In Max's case this took three sessions over five weeks.

In our first session, we looked at the broader issues in Max's life. He described his partner, their children, and his career path from school to his chosen work as a supervisor in a large window cleaning company. He told me about the sort of work he did, the equipment he used, and how although he supervised a small team of cleaners, it was a hands-on job in which he might do some of the more difficult work himself. He brought in snippets about the accident, but we were both clear that this was not the prolonged exposure to the memories that would follow "when he was ready". They could be described as excursions, where he was free to move in and out of the memory at will. He spontaneously mentioned he had been cleaning the windows of some retirement flats, that the fall was 15–18 feet, and the focal scene in nightmares and flashbacks was one of falling. Going off to sleep was particularly difficult because he felt falling sensations that would wake him with a jerk. He also mentioned "secondary flashbacks", still problematic but not as powerful as his memories of falling. These revolved around the moment he landed on the concrete. One thing that had really stuck with him had been the paramedic's comment about how lucky he had been – he kept imagining how much more serious it could have been.

I asked him to tell me a bit about his childhood. He described a rather unhappy upbringing in which Mum and Dad were divorced when he was one year old. He lived with his mother in the week and with his father at weekends. He said, "I remember thinking, 'I'm glad I'm not living with him.'" He was angry to have been moved to a school where he was parted from his friends and didn't work very hard. In terms of personality he felt he tended to hold things back and was a bit of a worrier. This was a good opportunity to discuss how much the proposed therapy would be going against his usual way of circumnavigating emotions. This was a useful discussion; he realized that facing difficulties would go against the grain, but was able to see how this "holding back" had not served him very well throughout his life. His partner often encouraged him to be more open and he felt she was right. He confirmed that he had cried "a bit" after the accident and had gone to his doctor, who gave him antidepressants and sleeping tablets.

Interspersed with our conversation were explanations about what would happen in therapy, and what impact this would have on him, in an attempt to get him realistically prepared and increase his motivation to stick with difficulties when they arose.

This session ended with him deciding to explain to his partner what treatment would involve and to continue reading my emotional processing book.

At the start of our second session I was greeted by a surprise. Max seemed to be very pleased with himself and announced that he had stopped smoking, inferring that I had been influential in this. Since I didn't even know he smoked and had not discussed smoking at all it was one of those odd surprises that you sometimes get during therapy. Generally he felt a lot better and less moody. He was still jumpy and sleeping poorly, but he was not thinking about his flashbacks as much. In the weeks between the sessions he had been preoccupied with his boss's reaction to his accident, again something hardly discussed until this point. "Why hadn't he bothered to find out how I am? It bothers me that he hasn't called. I worked so hard for my boss so why hasn't he bothered?"

Although Max was not facing his memories of the accident, this showed a definite attempt to process a difficult, but subsidiary, issue. Even though we had not reached the point when he felt "ready", he was already using the approach of facing difficult issues, which formerly had been brushed aside. He continued to talk quite intensely about this boss – all I needed to do was listen. Towards the end of the session he had reached a rather kindly re-appraisal about his boss's motives – "Maybe my boss has got PTSD or problems that make it difficult for him to visit me."

We spent the last twenty minutes of the session exploring what he was to expect from facing the traumatic memories, and how he could plan for this – for instance, what would he do if he found himself more irritable than usual with the children? His "homework" was to think through the implications of "opening up" more fully.

"After the last session," said Max at the start of our third session, "I've been thinking about it and wrote it down. I was down in the dumps thinking about it for a few days, but then I cheered up and stopped thinking about it. Later, when I read what I wrote it became clearer – the idea of letting it all out. I was quite relieved. I felt a big weight off my shoulders." I thought it was interesting that just making the decision to "go for it" lifted a weight off his shoulders. He hadn't entered that zone yet but was telling me his sleep was better and his partner had noticed this too.

Max then showed me what he had written about events after the accident – from the ambulance taking him to hospital, to being in the hospital, his meeting with various doctors and an anaesthetist, and his eight-hour operation. I could have simply taken it and read it but in terms of feeling emotions I thought it more relevant for Max to read his account to me. Yes, he had been engaging emotional memories as he had written this down, but speaking it out is a different modality and accesses the memory from another direction, and, remember, the *raison d'être* is to erode the power of a previously unaccessed emotional memory.

I was, however, slightly perplexed because I couldn't remember giving Max this homework. As with working through his reactions to his boss in the previous session, I think he was already embracing this new approach to facing emotions, but starting out with the more accessible points. Max started to read his account through to me like a BBC newsreader, pausing to look at me now and again to be sure he was engaging his audience. "Just be natural, Max," I interrupted, "don't try to put on a show for me. It's OK to make mistakes and it's OK to show your feelings." He loosened up a bit. His descriptions proved to be not simply a record of events but were quite emotional, including what he felt about the specialist saying "foreign objects in your wrists" and being amazed that surgery took eight hours. He had read in *Emotional Processing: Healing Through Feeling* an account of the difficulties in coming round after an operation and seemed quite excited about this, although I couldn't figure out why.

As we reached the end of this, our third session, I think we both realized that the next session would be the "big one".

Crunch Time

To the outsider, the start of our fourth session must have appeared rather odd. It was not particularly emotive or interpersonal, but rather an exercise in sorting out diaries and our availability for the next two sessions. The reason for this was the crucial nature of the timing of sessions at this point. When emotions are "red hot", continuity between sessions is crucial. Intervals of a week or less ensure that the crucial emotional processing can be both deep and continuous. After agreeing on the next two sessions, Max told me he had been discussing our last session at home with his partner and felt very supported.

"Are you ready to go through with it?"

"Yes, it's now or never."

"OK, I'd like you to take me through what happened, starting when you got up on the morning of the accident. Take me through everything in detail. Is that OK? Don't hold back, and if you feel like crying, do. Showing your feelings is OK."

So Max began.

He woke up at 6.45 a.m. on the Wednesday of the accident and had a hot drink and a cigarette, then a bit of toast, and went upstairs to wash. It was a dry, light morning, and he drove to work listening to 2CR, a local radio station.

What has this got to do with his accident? The answer is we are trying to recreate the total memory in as much detail as possible – memory joggers such as the weather, what was eaten for breakfast, and what songs were playing all help to set the scene.

He got to work, but his colleague, Lenny, was five minutes late. They set up the van together, ensuring that all the right equipment was in place, and drove to the nursing home, which was their first job of the day. Max described his route and the state of the traffic. He remembered thinking, "I'd like to finish early today so I can get home." He described the building they were to clean and how he and Lenny started off by cleaning the basement floors, planning to "meet in the middle". "Lenny was a slow learner, but a nice guy. We were to meet in the middle, but he was nowhere near that when I got there." He described how he placed the ladders to start on the first floor windows, then some of the second floor ones before stopping for a packed lunch.

After lunch, Max got back to work again. He described the rather odd shape of a balcony on the second floor near the roof where he was working. The balcony was not rectangular but had slanting sides. He had been washing windows on this floor for about five minutes when he put his right foot back to where he thought the balcony floor was and started to fall. "I saw windows zoom past me. I'm falling. Will I die? What will be at the bottom?" It was difficult for Max to talk about these crucial seconds but he approached it with determination. "My heart was racing, I was sweating. Horror. I remember lying on the ground sweating, as if someone had hit me round the head with a plank. My ears were ringing and dull. My mate came rushing up and said did I need an ambulance. He offered me a cigarette." Max had landed on his wrist, and he remembered seeing a finger sticking up unnaturally in an impossible position. His memories at this point were concertinaed together. Someone in the crowd said, "Don't move him," and in the ambulance on the way to hospital he remembered thinking tearfully, "I might not be there for my children. What if I never come home – what if I never see my children again?" By this time Max, who generally tried to put on a cheery front, had a serious look I had never seen before.

He had really done an excellent job of doggedly going through all the details of the accident, and as far as I could see had not held back when it came to the most horrific moments. I told him how well he had done, and we carried out a sort of debriefing of the session. He described how difficult the session had been, how his hands were wet and his mouth dry in describing what had happened. "As I described it I became more upset and found it really difficult going on. Thinking about the fall, there was a black bit."

After he had regained his composure we agreed that a useful homework exercise would be to write this down, concentrating on the fall and what he thought and felt during the fall. We had of course pre-planned the next session, and, still a little dazed and without his usual smile, Max left the office.

It's strange what you feel after patients leave the therapy office. In a way, I too had shared in his moment of intense horror as he fell from the roof. Before the session it was his private catastrophe – he had not shared the emotional moment with anyone else. Now I too knew exactly what he felt and thought during the accident. It is not easy seeing someone sweat it out, but I knew from countless other cases what dramatic changes can result from this simple re-telling. How would Max be next time? We had discussed together how many times he might need to re-tell the story. He was aware it could be several sessions. When asked directly I had told him it was a bit difficult to predict. Sometimes twice is enough, but often it is many more times than this as people focus on and recall different aspects of the trauma, and, again, it depends on the severity, complexity, and repeated nature of the trauma. Max had a lot in his favour – he was highly motivated, understood the therapy well, had a very supportive partner who was prepared to discuss it with him, and he had already made his own successful attempts at understanding his boss's reactions and what happened in hospital after the accident.

After the Storm

In the next session I was keen to see how Max was faring. "I went home and felt relieved," he started. "I felt relieved and emotional – I still do. I was remembering more in my sleep, but not actually waking up as in nightmares. According to my partner I wasn't jumping about this week."

He continued, "I feel the tears at the back of my eyes that want to flood out. They have flooded out – on Saturday evening. Elsa comforted me. It was like a burden on me and now I've actually talked about it I feel better."

However, he felt more irritable than before. He reported that he had made a start on writing it down, but had not got very far because his daughter had been unwell and required a lot of attention.

In this session there was no sharp intake of breath; he began the narrative with rather a workmanlike inevitability. He repeated his account of the accident unusually, starting off by saying, "It was a lovely place, scenery round the back and all lawns, stripy and very long." In this account I asked him for a very detailed account of the fall – exactly what he remembered happening, what he felt and thought. I tried to engage kinaesthetic memory, that is, I got him to stand up and make the actual movements he made when he fell and to lie down exactly in the way he had fallen. Often this accesses new aspects of the total emotional memory. He drew a (very neat) picture of the balcony, showing from where he had fallen.

At the end of this he repeated something I had told him in an earlier session as if he had finally got it this time. "A memory can't break an arm," he said, pretty pleased with himself.

I asked him to go through the events once more, then twice silently to recall the event in real time. Obviously in a real fall no one is talking to a therapist so that introduces an unreal element. Going through it in real time without having to speak accesses even more of the memory. "I've never done this before," he said.

We had left a two to three week gap before our sixth session. Three days after our last session, he had written about the sequel to the fall which "started flowing out and I didn't feel emotional". He said he had done this together with his partner. Over three sittings in three nights they had worked on it together. He had talked with her freely, in a detail he had never done before. She said, "Well done," after he had finished. He reported his sleep pattern was back to normal; he had not woken up in a sweat with any bad dreams, and his exaggerated startle was "not there any more". He had resumed going to the social club and started playing snooker again, and felt his playing was good – "better than my friends". His recovery had speeded up, I think, because he had shared so much with his partner in the interim.

We again went through the accident, this time concentrating on events in hospital. He had been shocked when a doctor had suggested he might "lose his hands".

I asked him at the end of the session how it had been talking about the accident, which he felt was "fine". I pushed it a bit too far when I said, "Did you want to talk about it?" "No, I didn't" was the honest reply.

We agreed a full month before session seven and then two months to session eight, the last session. Max's progress had been so quick I left long intervals to make absolutely sure his progress was stable. Sessions took much the same form as before, repeating those sections of the accident where emotional issues still existed. This was not so much a whole emotional landscape but rather small but poignant issues that still hung around. He experienced strong pockets of emotion when discussing the topic of his wrists. He described how seeing his black and yellow arms and pins in his wrists was "disgusting – I looked away". He worried at the time because none of the specialists could tell him how much function he was likely to regain.

In the last session I asked him about thoughts and flashbacks of his injuries. His reply showed the extent to which he had processed the traumatic memories. "If I sit down and think I can remember bits. Before, it was always on my mind. Before, I couldn't get it out of my mind; now I have to think about it in order to get it on my mind."

His recovery had been so marked that I felt I needed more proof of the effect. I was almost certain he wasn't just telling me what I wanted to hear. Could he be exaggerating? So for the sake of completeness and for an accurate report to send to Knighton-Royal about the therapy, I asked Max to repeat the same psychometric assessment scales as before.

The Davidson Trauma Scale,[1] a measure of the likelihood of having PTSD, scored as follows:

	At assessment (7 September 2007)	At therapy session 8 (7 July 2008)
Intrusion Score	29	0
Avoidance/Numbing Score	18	0
Hyperarousal Score	28	1
Total Score	75	1
	(extremely high probability of a diagnosis of PTSD)	(extremely low probability of a diagnosis of PTSD)

A psychometric symptoms scale (Foulds and Bedford DSSI)[2] showed six out of seven anxiety symptoms and four out of seven depression symptoms at assessment. This had changed to no anxiety or depressive symptoms after therapy.

A self-esteem scale (Rosenberg)[3] showed moderately poor self-esteem at assessment and high normal self-esteem after therapy.

A quality of life scale showed impairment in home management, social activities, private leisure activities, family relationships, and sexual relationship before therapy. Now the only area which Max still reported as somewhat restricted was work, but he had got a date to start training for his new chosen occupation, plumbing. "During the time it all happened, I asked myself 'Why me?'" said Max. "All I think about now is the future and I'm quite looking forward to it."

Chapter 12

Preparing for Therapy

Here are some of the typical benefits of Emotional Processing Therapy:

- Disturbing reminders of the trauma lose their emotional strength. Nightmares and flashbacks can be eradicated.
- Memories will not be triggered so easily and, if they are, will not be as frightening.
- Sleep will improve.
- Memory and concentration will improve.
- The person will feel less hyped up.
- The person's mood will lift. Anxiety, panic, and depression should reduce.
- The person will not need to self-medicate to keep symptoms under control (either by prescribed medication, alcohol, or illicit drugs).
- The person will be able to get on with their life and personal development rather than be stuck in a "slough of despond".
- The person's social, work, sex, and leisure life should be much improved.

I have used the word "overcome" in the subtitle of this book. Total recovery from PTSD is possible, and the person can even show "Post Traumatic Growth". Recovery cannot be guaranteed because it depends on a complex mix of factors such as the type and severity of the trauma, whether loved ones were injured or killed, whether it has left them physically disabled, financially disadvantaged, without a job, and so on. The therapy cannot change life factors such as these but it can deal with most of the Post Traumatic Stress symptoms.

There is one *but*. All these benefits can *ultimately* emerge when the therapy has run its course. Unfortunately the therapy itself is not easy and may *increase* distress, *increase* intrusive thoughts, and *increase* the symptoms of PTSD before there is relief. It involves facing the fear head on – or, as it were, going into the eye of the storm. For this reason it doesn't suit everyone, or circumstances may just not be right at this time. The treatment holds great healing promise but at a personal cost.

Preparing for Self-Help Therapy

Although self-help does hold much promise, there are a number of precautions to consider. One of the biggest drawbacks is that the therapy requires the person to talk in detail and at length about their trauma experiences, and this can be exhausting, frightening, and intensely painful. It is often hard to find the right person prepared to listen at length and to keep the sufferer motivated to go on when they hit a black spot. So, if you want to "go it alone", here is what you need:

a) one or two close friends or relatives prepared to listen to you, a lot

b) a supportive social climate around you – people who care for you

c) friends or family members who understand what is involved during the therapy and know what to expect during the worst time; sufferers can become more irritable, more moody, and more fearful as they bring out their difficult memories

d) to make careful preparation about how to handle situations – for instance, what you would do if you become more irritated than normal with your children

e) a willingness to accept mental pain and persist through bad times

f) to keep a record to remind yourself of progress and provide encouragement through bad times

g) to know where to get help if you hit problems

h) to know how to handle setbacks, which are a normal and

inevitable index that you are trying; "error-less" learning is vary rare, so expect dips in progress

i) to know when to stop if it is not working.

One thing to remember, though, and this is rather like the casket analogy in Chapter 5: once you open a can of worms, it is nasty. It cannot easily be closed again. The promise of the end result is terrific, but don't start something you can't see through.

Seeking Out a Therapist

If it is clear that the reader is suffering from Post Traumatic Stress Disorder, my general advice is for them to seek out psychological help either through the public health system or by seeing a therapist on a private basis. Post Traumatic Stress Disorder is not easy to treat and the results of self-help cannot be guaranteed. Even with professional help, not every psychological therapist, counsellor, or cognitive behavioural therapist can successfully treat it. Personally I think it is important to seek out someone who has both detailed knowledge of PTSD, a specialist if you like, and a sound knowledge of psychological treatment principles. I must confess that when I first started treating patients with PTSD in the 1980s I was not very effective. Patients might improve to a certain level, but then progress would plateau, leaving them with significant distress by the end of therapy. It was only after I started to see case after case of people suffering from PTSD and it became my principle workload that I really got to understand the dynamics of the trauma experience.

The other factor is the nature of the treatment provided; for the majority of sufferers, therapy that involves the systematic facing of traumatic memories has been shown to be the most effective psychological treatment to date.[1, 2, 3] The treatment, although highly effective, can be distressing, and the therapist should make preparations with the patient to help them cope with and maximize therapy. If the therapist is not fully convinced of the benefits of facing traumatic memories, or has not seen patients completely relieved of their distress by the therapy, they may be reluctant to guide patients through the emotional turmoil. There are many different psychological therapies available for various conditions, and since PTSD sufferers may have other problems too, treatment can end up concentrating on relationship issues, self-esteem, work stress, and so on, leaving the traumatic memories untouched by the end. Of course patients will be assisted in whatever emphasis the therapy takes, but the core of their PTSD symptoms will remain if not properly accessed.

There is quite a perplexing array of therapists out there, but I would seek out:

- a qualified clinical psychologist (in the UK, working in the National Health Service as a qualified clinical psychologist or recognized by their professional body, the Health Professions Council, as a chartered clinical psychologist)
- one with a specialist knowledge of trauma
- a therapist trained in using Emotional Processing Therapy, otherwise known as Exposure Based Therapy, Prolonged Exposure or Trauma Focused Therapy. This is a variant of Cognitive Behaviour Therapy (CBT). CBT is such an umbrella term for a variety of different treatment approaches that someone trained in CBT will not necessarily have Trauma Focused Therapy skills. On the other hand they might have these skills. So, a qualified cognitive behaviour therapist might be appropriate (in the UK they would be recognized by the British Association of Behavioural and Cognitive Psychotherapy).

Generally, counsellors, psychotherapists, NLP (Neuro Linguistic Programming) specialists, hypnotherapists, or various complementary therapists, would not primarily be using a Trauma Focused approach, so would not be an obvious choice.

Who Should *Not* Start a Self-Help Programme?

Edna Foa and her colleagues from the University of Pennsylvania have extensively researched PTSD therapy and, in their book *Prolonged Exposure Therapy for PTSD*,[4, 5] document situations in which the therapy should not be used:

a) if the person is currently suicidal

b) if the person has recently purposely injured themself (by cutting or burning themself for instance)

c) if they are currently experiencing a psychotic illness (schizophrenia or manic depression)

d) if they are at high risk of being assaulted (for instance, living with domestic violence). Foa and colleagues state: "If your client is currently in a living situation in which he or she is being beaten, sexually assaulted, or seriously harmed, insuring safety or removal from the dangerous situations should be the focus of intervention. Safety is paramount." The conditions are just not right for a challenging therapy like this. Once the client is settled into a safe environment the treatment would be appropriate.

Why Not Let Sleeping Dogs Lie?

What is all this fuss about facing the traumatic memory? Isn't it best just to let the memories lie there, and not stir them up? Shouldn't psychologists just concentrate on improving the positive strengths of individuals or teach them better ways to control unwanted thoughts and nightmares?

What are the underlying reasons for bringing out and facing distressing traumatic memories? When someone's life is threatened in a way that creates "intense fear, helplessness, or horror", the whole experience is charged with unusually high levels of negative emotion. When the memory of the experience is stored, it will not just be a record of objective events, but a memory of the negative emotions too. As mentioned in Chapter 6, it will be a hot memory, supercharged with horror, fear, and dismay. If you can imagine the red-hot lava bubbling inside a volcano, that would represent such a memory. It is primarily an emotion-bound memory, governed by emotional rules rather than by the rules of logic, that is, as long as the memory remains suppressed, away from the light of reason and logic. The following table shows how the memory is stored (on the left) and how it changes when brought out and talked about (on the right).

Characteristics of the Unprocessed Hot Memory	Changes When the Memory is Discussed
1. Stored as a highly charged emotional memory.	After discussion, re-stored in a "colder" way.
2. Stored in emotional symbolism referred to by Freud as "Primary Process", i.e. stored more in the "illogical" language of dreams.	More logical cause and effect connections made, and re-stored in more logical mode.
3. Events are unexplained, loosely organized or disconnected, i.e. confused memory.	More connections made. Memory organized better.
4. Random, illogical connections are not challenged.	Illogical ideas are invalidated and evaporate, e.g. the idea that they might be injured again if they talk about it.
5. The unresolved emotional power of the memory creates mental tension.	Release of emotional feeling (catharsis).
6. The unresolved memory absorbs much mental resource, diverting mental attention, and distorts mental balance.	The resolution of elements of the memory reduces the demand on mental resource and restores a better mental balance.
7. Without exposure, the memory remains emotionally charged.	With exposure, habituation occurs (reduction of the emotional charge of the memory).
8. The memory remains unchanged.	Each time it is discussed, it changes a bit.

A red-hot memory will not automatically improve with time alone, just as a volcano retains its power. The memory needs to be accessed, brought out, thought about. The memory then doesn't go back in the same "hot" environment. It is re-stored in a more organized and less emotionally charged way.

Is it Possible to Treat Dissociation?

Memory Dissociation

Kenneth had been on the top floor of a hotel in Italy that was destroyed by fire. His room had been surrounded by fire, which was beginning to come through the floorboards. Being a narrow old building, there was no escape other than the narrow stairways engulfed by fire. He miraculously escaped by smashing through a window in his room and surviving a 40-foot fall. He was referred to me by his General Practitioner nine years later for a course of psychological therapy. He had been suffering from Post Traumatic Stress Disorder over the nine years. This had severely affected his ability to work and he was now registered as homeless. He was tormented by nightmares of fires and death. He could remember the events leading up to the fire and waking up after his escape in an Italian hospital. He had no memory of the most traumatic part of the experience and no idea how he escaped. He did, however, have a vague recollection or dream of waking up in a smoke-filled room but didn't know whether this was real or imagined. He was desperate for help with his nightmares – he felt his lack of sleep disrupted nearly every area of his life. I explained to Kenneth the general approach of facing distressing memories and that it would be especially difficult if he recalled a new "buried" memory. He felt the approach made so much sense and he had a real determination to beat his "demon". One of the potential problems with an Exposure Based Therapy approach was the lack of any close relatives to support him during the therapy; however, we were able to arrange for his social worker, who was fully briefed about the therapy, to provide extra support, and we could talk over the phone if problems emerged.

We spent several sessions going over events leading up to the fire the night before, and his extensive stay in hospital afterwards. This helped him to understand the approach and put together what had happened in hospital. His homework took on the appearance of a major research project, contacting the Italian police, fire brigade, newspapers, the hospital, and Embassy staff for accounts and records of what happened to help fill in the gaps. But this reached a limit when it came to his experience of the fire itself – all he had was the snippet of a memory – a recurrent dream of waking up in a smoke-filled room. I said, "We're not sure if this is just a dream or part of an actual recollection, but let's work with it, trying to make your best guess as to what happened." It was likely that, as he put together his imagined ideas, he might jog an element of the real memory. As we talked, he thought his inclination would have been to open the door, and, yes, he actually did remember being on the landing. He thinks he tried to go down the narrow stairs, but gave up. He did remember going up a few steps to the base of the next set of stairs then retreating to his room. In the next session he had recalled that there were two American students upstairs and he remembered shouting up to them from these stairs. We worked with half memories, probabilities, intuitions, actual memories, piecing together what might have happened. At the same time, he was receiving translations of reports from the Embassy and the Italian police, and had two newspaper reports with pictures of the blaze. He was able to triangulate what was in the written reports with his memory, as it shaped up. For instance, the pictures of the blazing hotel and his memory of the wall of another building about 4 feet from his window, and the nature of the injuries to his arm and head suggested that he had jumped out of the window and hit the other building as he fell. Through this process we put together an almost complete picture of events with many new and individual memories helping to make a coherent record of events. He was pleased to have pieced together what had confused and perplexed him before, and the detailed repetition of the (probable) memories of being trapped in his room had a beneficial impact on his nightmares. He was planning to start work again on a part-time basis and felt more confident about the future.

Dissociation and Emotional Experience

Paula did not have dissociated memories as Kenneth had; she could recall everything that had happened to her after she was diagnosed with breast cancer. She would recall what the surgeon said, what she did next, her surgery, chemotherapy, and radiotherapy. What was missing was the emotional reaction to events. When the surgeon first told her that she had cancer he was amazed at her lack of reaction, and asked her whether she had understood what he said. She told Lin, the cancer specialist nurse, and me that her reaction to having cancer, and her whole journey from then on, was numb, and that "I haven't begun to deal with it." As we talked more with Paula it transpired that this was not the first time she had failed to feel emotion at significant events. Sadly, her story went back to when she was six years old, when her family used to regularly visit her uncle and aunt in Nottingham. This was the start of a series of incidents of sexual abuse until she flatly refused to go on the visits at eleven years old. When her parents finally discovered what was happening, it led to a huge family battle with the uncle that still rumbles on today.

Paula, who could not escape the inevitable abuse in the early years, had started to become emotionally numb and detached at every visit to Nottingham and this type of reaction became more common at other times too, when there was any stress at home, with friends, or at school. Her normal emotional development had been disrupted by incomprehensible and painful sexual abuse. Paula was relieved to have shared the outline of what happened with us. After discussion of the role of emotional processing in therapy and having read *Emotional Processing: Healing Through Feeling*, she agreed with the idea of dealing with the sexual abuse first in therapy before tackling her cancer experiences. Over the next four sessions she shared with Lin details of the sexual abuse and began to understand not just the roots of her dissociated feelings (numbness and detachment) but also how it had had a ripple effect on the rest of her emotional life, her self esteem, closeness to others, her over-eating and attempts to make herself look unattractive. When I saw her five sessions later she felt she had really understood the effects of the abuse on her now, and the sparkle and new sense of humour showed that something had happened.

Though she had made progress, Paula confessed that "it's as if I've totally put the cancer on hold." She knew from her session talking about sexual abuse that strong emotional feelings could suddenly "click in" as she mentioned unpleasant details of the abuse and knew the same would happen when she started to open up about cancer. Paula, Lin, and I had a long discussion about the best way to approach therapy from now on. As a first step, Paula agreed to write a detailed account of what happened, allowing herself to feel any emotions that might be stirring.

At the next session Paula was surprised by the exercise because what she thought had been no emotional response, when explored by writing about it like this, proved to be incorrect. She devised her own notation of putting in bold any emotional experience. This record was the start of a successful programme in which her emotional experiences and understanding has blossomed, showing the possibilities for helping dissociated emotions. Here is part of Paula's record:

Before Diagnosis

*When I first noticed a lump I thought it would go away on its own
and **so wasn't that worried**. When I noticed the discharge from
my nipple **I began to realize it was probably more serious**
and, as I'd left it about a week, I was **concerned enough to
make an appointment** to see a doctor. When the doctor told
me she thought it was a fluid-filled cyst, I felt **relieved**. When
she then said that, due to our family's cancer history, she wanted
to send me to the hospital for a mammogram, **I felt a bit more
apprehensive** but grateful that it was being checked out.*

*When I went for the ultrasound I noticed the lady highlighting
areas on the screen and there was something about **her body
language** that **made me nervous**. Looking back now, it was
probably **at that point that I knew I had something more
sinister** – the fact that I was sent an appointment for a biopsy
soon after (on a Wednesday) confirmed it. I took my sister with me
to the hospital for the biopsy. We were **both quiet**, a sign I now
recognize was realization that bad news was coming.*

*The biopsy was, to this day, one **of the worst experiences**
I've ever had. The machine used to take tissue made a sound like
a stapler and I made the biggest mistake of looking at the screen to
see a huge needle in my breast. I knew I was going to faint and tried
to warn them by saying 'I feel faint' and next thing I remember is
waking up to a load of worried nurses standing over me, one holding
a fan trying to cool me down. When I was well enough, I went back
to the cubicle to change and that's when **I saw my face**. It was
totally grey, no colour at all. It triggered a memory back to mum
in the funeral parlour, I looked like mum. **I looked dead**. That
freaked me out a lot, and I actually remember looking at myself
a lot when I was getting changed because I couldn't believe I was
that colour.*

*On the Saturday, I had a call from the registrar to inform me
that I had an appointment with Mr S. on the following Tuesday
late afternoon and to confirm I could attend. When I said I could,
he explained that he was worried I wouldn't get the appointment
in the post in time, hence his phone call. I thought afterwards that
it was strange for him to be calling me on a weekend and **that's
when I knew I had cancer**. I called Lorraine [her sister] to let
her know about the appointment with Mr S. and she said she would*

come with me. On Sunday, Lorraine asked me what I was expecting to hear on Tuesday and I said 'that I've got breast cancer' and she agreed.

Diagnosis

*I remember being **very quiet in the car with Lorraine, unusual for us**. At the hospital we got ourselves a drink and waited. We were **laughing in the waiting room** at the choice of music on the tape machine. When I was called in and told I had a tumour in my left breast, **it wasn't shock, it was relief that I knew**. I asked what happened next and Mr S. asked me if I understood. I told him we were expecting it and just wanted **to know** what happened from here on in. [As Paula read out this account it was at this point that she started crying.] I remember thinking that I **had to wait for the operation** and **thought that was strange because surely it could spread more in that time** but didn't say anything. As it turned out, I only had to wait just over a week anyway.*

It would appear that it is possible to apply the same general emotional processing principles to dissociated experience with successful results. Although it is perhaps harder for individuals, it is as important to process deeply hidden material as it is to process material more easily available to consciousness.

Chapter 13

Emotional Processing Style

Something has to happen before therapy begins. It is more to do with lifestyle than with the trauma as such. It is not to do with diet, calorie intake, vitamins, eating too much saturated fat, or whether we have our five fruit and veg a day. It is not to do with exercise, whether aerobic, muscle toning, or simply burning up excess calories. The media seem to love self-improvement of the body in terms of make-up, cosmetic surgery, or getting the perfect wardrobe to present the best image of our body. It is not that either. It is not mental toning or calming the mind through relaxation, yoga, or meditation. Neither is it sleep management, money management, time management, or any other management. It is something that Max (see Chapter 11) began to discover early in therapy and proved to be an essential aspect of his recovery. The crucial part of preparation for therapy is for the person to evaluate their own emotional processing style. In the first sessions, when Max described his upbringing and how he typically handled life's ups and downs, he realized how much he "held back", not wishing to face emotional difficulties or talk about his feelings too much. His partner had often encouraged him to open up. Max had a typical style of handling, or in his case, not handling, emotions. He needed to re-examine this and change his approach in order to facilitate the therapy process. If he had wished to continue his usual style of "circumnavigating" emotions, it would be very strange for him to come to sessions in which I was encouraging him to face his distressing memories, only to return home to a reversed style of emotional living. Therapy would have been pulling against the tide all the way – and ultimately may not have been successful.

As it was, Max made a complete recovery from the symptoms of PTSD, but was also much happier about the more open emotional style with which he related to his partner and children.

This is where we need to reach for and dust off our "emotion rulebook". An emotion rulebook may sound strange. It is a sort of emotions operational manual with complicated implicit rules for how to feel emotions and how to express them to others. Unfortunately we can't pick up our manual and read the rules that easily; they are implicitly written in our brains by the hand of life's experiences. If you put your rulebook down and accidentally picked up the wrong rulebook, let's say, of someone from Mexico (assuming you are not already Mexican), then you might get quite a surprise at how much physically closer you wanted to be to others, how much more you wanted to share your feelings, to be part of the group and no longer need to have your "personal space" (with my apologies for the cultural stereotypes). Our culture plays a part in our rulebook, but within every culture there is also much variation. Families differ in what they consider normal emotions, and there are clearly variations in different family members too.

To get a glimpse of what our rulebook has in it we need to think of the family in which we were brought up. How did our mother and our father react to situations? Did they keep quiet, talk it over, fly off the handle? Did our parents differ in their emotional responses? How did they respond to each other? How did they react to me? Did it differ from reactions to my brothers and sisters? What was expected of me and what was definitely not expected? Our parents themselves would have had sets of beliefs about emotional conduct forged throughout their own lives, influenced in turn by their family, which can get handed down the generations. What is in your emotional rulebook about crying? Is crying OK for girls but not boys? OK for others but not you? OK at home but not at work? OK for serious but not minor things? OK alone but not with others? OK if tears of happiness but not sadness? What about touch – is it OK to be touched, to touch others – who, when, how? There are many permutations and combinations.

"I don't understand what you are getting at" was the reaction of one client to my discussion on rulebooks in an emotional processing group. "I didn't really know my father much so I don't think he had much influence, but mother was perfect."

"How do you mean?" I asked.

"She was totally loving and giving. Kissed and cuddled me, made me feel important and loved, and basically met my every need." This was all excellent and it showed in the way that this person was caring and supportive of the others in the group too. But as the group members explored this more, she did come to realize that there was a negative side to this. Her mother had spent so much time arranging for her to have a perfect life, without stress, that as an adult she also tried too much to control her own destiny, so that life had to continually have a happy hue with no black clouds on the horizon. She realized how much control she tried to exert over her own mental environment, trying to blank out unhappy feelings and generate nice feelings all the time. Others were affected too – her children refused to let her have the TV remote control because of her censorship of anything negative. Max was more straightforward in "holding back" emotions. This client was open and sharing but mentally manipulated her world to maximize happiness and avoid negative emotions.

Parents and families are of course not the only influences in life. For instance, school life and school friends also help to shape the emotional world of the adolescent.

I suppose a key question is "Is it OK to have negative feelings?" or "What is my reaction to experiencing strong emotions?"

Reading Your Emotion Rulebook

I mentioned how difficult it is to read our own emotion rulebook, so to help the process I have included a short self-assessment questionnaire that provides information about a person's emotional processing style. It provides some indication of areas of our emotion rulebook that might become problematic. I say "might" because it depends how well life treats you. It might be possible for someone with a problematic emotional processing style to cope well in life if not confronted by trauma or serious stress. On the other hand, someone with the most honed and polished emotional processing style might collapse under the weight of too great a trauma. Emotional processing style is one important factor determining our resistance to life's threats and stresses.

The emotional processing research team at Bournemouth University and NHS Trusts in Dorset have devised a way of assessing emotional processing style called the Emotional Processing Scale (EPS). The background to this is described in the chapter entitled

"The Idea Behind the Science" in *Emotional Processing: Healing Through Feeling*.[1] Many popular magazines provide questionnaires on psychological characteristics, such as "Inner strength", "Attractiveness to the opposite sex", "Are you the marrying type?" devised between coffee break and lunchtime. Psychometrics is a field of psychological science with its own set of principles and practices about the scientific development of questionnaires. It takes many years to develop a validated questionnaire, in this case, eight years. Emotional processing style, as measured by the Emotional Processing Scale, has been shown to relate to anxiety, depression, PTSD, eating disorders, chronic fatigue, pain and even colorectal cancer.[2, 3, 4, 5, 6, 7]

The assessment that follows, the "Condensed Emotional Processing Scale", is a shorter version of the EPS, produced specifically for this book. The purpose of this version is to give an initial indication of what is involved in an emotion rulebook, and whether there are any problems that need attention. Whereas the full Emotional Processing Scale[8] is a properly validated research tool, this version is for illustrative purposes only.

The Condensed Emotional Processing Scale has twelve questions and two boxes to fill in. It is based on the person's emotions and feelings in the last week only (in order to encourage a more accurate memory of events).

Next there is the scoring key. The Condensed Emotional Processing Scale measures six different emotional dimensions plus the Total Emotional Processing Score, and each dimension needs to be separately scored. One dimension, "attunement", is reverse scored to bring it into line with all the other dimensions. The higher the scores, the more problematic the emotional processing style will be.

Lastly, there is a traffic light scheme for interpreting the scores on the different dimensions; scores that fall in the green area indicate a healthy style of processing, scores in the amber area indicate that there might be problems, and scores in the red area indicate a problem. This is based on data from about 600 healthy individuals, pain sufferers, and those referred for psychological therapy. Remember, the scale is provided more to illustrate the different dimensions than to provide a diagnosis. If you have a high score this relates to your emotional processing style – it is not an indication of mental problems. A high score indicates a style that makes a person vulnerable to psychological problems, not that they have those problems currently.

The Condensed Emotional Processing Scale

INSTRUCTIONS

The idea of this questionnaire is to try to understand something about your emotions and feelings. In order to fill it in, you will need to fix the last week firmly in your mind.

First of all spend a few minutes thinking back over what you have been doing in the last week. Starting from one week ago today, try to think about where you were, what you were doing, who you met, anything you may remember. If you have a diary, check for any appointments or reminders of each day.

With the last week in mind, what would you say was the most frequent positive or pleasant emotion that you felt?

With the last week in mind, what would you say was the most frequent negative or unpleasant emotion that you felt?

The following questionnaire now lists different descriptions of how you may have felt or acted last week. This refers to your feelings in general, not just your most frequent emotions as you have just filled in. After each description say how much you agree that the description applied to you last week, ranging from completely disagree to completely agree.

	completely disagree	disagree	in between	agree	completely agree
1. I kept quiet about my feelings.					
2. I bottled up my emotions.					
3. My emotional reactions lasted for more than a day.					
4. I tended to repeatedly experience the same emotions.					
5. When upset or angry it was difficult to control what I said.					
6. I reacted too much to what people said or did.					
7. I tried very hard to avoid things that might make me upset.					
8. I could not tolerate unpleasant feelings.					
9. I switched off my feelings.					
10. There seemed to be a big blank in my feelings.					
11. By taking notice of my feelings it helped me to make better choices and decisions.					
12. I was able to link my feelings to things that happened to me in the past week.					

Are there any important things you would like to add?

```



```

Thank you for filling in this questionnaire.

Scoring Key for Condensed Emotional Processing Scale

The scale measures six dimensions, each with two questions assigned to it. They are:

Suppression (questions 1 & 2)
Signs of unprocessed emotion (questions 3 & 4)
Emotional over-reactivity (questions 5 & 6)
Avoidance (questions 7 & 8)
Dissociation (questions 9 & 10)
Attunement (questions 11 & 12)

The total scale adds together the six subscales. The higher the score, the more problematic the emotional processing style will be.

The "positive" and "negative" emotions boxes are there to help you focus on the last week, but also to try to consider what emotions fill your life the most. Why these emotions? What is behind this? Were these the most frequent feelings simply because of the events last week, or are these fairly typical of your life? Sometimes people don't directly write down an emotion such as "anxiety", "feeling buoyant", "happy", but write down events that may have given them emotions, e.g. "went to a birthday party with my daughter". This might suggest the need to distinguish their own inner feelings from external events that generate feelings, so the question in this case would be, "Do I need to understand my emotions better?"

Scoring Key

Q	completely disagree	disagree	in between	agree	completely agree	Subscore (add the scores of the two questions)	Name of dimension
1	0	1	2	3	4		Suppression
2	0	1	2	3	4		
3	0	1	2	3	4		Signs of unprocessed emotion
4	0	1	2	3	4		
5	0	1	2	3	4		Emotional over-reactivity
6	0	1	2	3	4		
7	0	1	2	3	4		Avoidance
8	0	1	2	3	4		
9	0	1	2	3	4		Dissociation
10	0	1	2	3	4		
11	4	3	2	1	0		Attunement
12	4	3	2	1	0		
				Total Score (0–48)			

"Suppression" and "avoidance" are styles of emotional coping that are often a problem in PTSD – a person high in these scores may attempt to control emotional memories too much. "Dissociation" reflects a stronger level of cutting off of emotions, which usually happens subconsciously. "Signs of unprocessed emotion" suggest the person is going through a time of stress and their experiences are not yet processed – this is usually high with psychological problems generally, as well as in PTSD. "Attunement" is a positive valuing of one's emotional experience, regarded as a positive style of processing. "Over-reactivity" is the sense of not being in control of one's emotions and their expression. Scores that are too high in "over-reactivity" may be problematic as well as scores that are too low (not enough reaction). The Total Emotional Processing Score is the best index of problems in emotional processing style.

Interpretation of Condensed Emotional Processing Scale Scores

The traffic light scoring system.

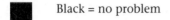 Black = no problem

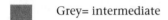 Grey= intermediate

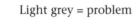 Light grey = problem

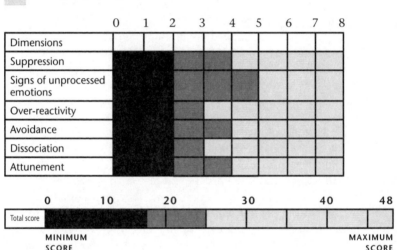

Should We Listen to Emotions?

I have concentrated rather a lot on the negative aspects of problems in emotional processing style, but what are the positive benefits of a more accepting approach to emotions?

- To know oneself better. Emotions usually exist for a reason. Listening to feelings provides information that helps in understanding oneself better.
- To reduce tension and improve concentration. Suppressing emotions requires much psychological energy.
- To feel better. Working in harmony with oneself is so much easier than struggling to control feelings.

- To improve the quality of positive emotions. By trying to dampen negative feelings, positive ones often become subdued too. Less regulation allows more spontaneous colour in emotional life.
- To improve health. Internal battles with oneself may have physical repercussions such as depleting the immune system. Better physical health may well be a consequence of better emotional processing style.
- To improve relationships with others. Being more open about feelings, negative as well as positive, can mean others get to know you better and understand who you are.
- To maximize our "emotional immune system". Emotions are quite safe and can find their own balance without too much control and interference from us.
- Registering and listening to emotions does not necessarily mean expressing the emotion. But it does provide an information base for the person to decide what is best to do. Not listening to emotions in effect means having no information or a confused information base.
- Emotions are an essential part of a person, as is their reason and judgment. Both emotion and reason work best in harmony with each other rather than one predominating. The "stiff upper lip" really refers to the dominance of reason over emotion. "Hysterical" usually refers to the dominance of emotion over reason. Somewhere in between must lie a happy medium for most of us.

Chapter 14

Facing the Memories

In a way the treatment idea is very simple. The traumatic memories are unprocessed, causing many emotional problems; they need to be processed. The memories are the cause of the problem and facing them is the answer. You can use this simple idea to guide the course of your own therapy. You need to concentrate on unprocessed memories. Once they are no longer troublesome, they could be described as "processed," and the exercise can move on to other unprocessed memories. Therapy finishes when the person can think about and talk about their trauma and carry out activities related to their trauma without distress.

The Principles of Memory Processing

Before actually facing traumatic memories, I'd like to explain some of the principles of how to do this.

Accessing the memories. The memories need to be brought out – not just thought about but expressed in some way, whether verbally or in writing, or both. At first only part of the memories may appear but ultimately all of them should be brought out.

Accessing the memories in detail. This is not a matter of recalling the broad facts of what happened but of accessing the memories in great detail, creating a second-by-second account, dealing with minor things, such as smelling the breath of the paramedic as they leaned over; not just the objectively "important" details. These are personal memories – how it affected you – not a police constable's account of what happened. Everything you thought and felt, everything said by you and others, are the crucial parts of what needs to be accessed. This is where someone else – a therapist or friend – can be very useful because they can ask questions, such as "What did you think when you smelled the paramedic's breath?"

Accessing the memories in as many sense modalities as possible. This is not just memorizing events visually; sounds, smells, and tastes can be very important. Memorizing the physical pain and your emotions and thoughts are crucial too. Kinaesthetic sense – that is, the movements your body made – are part of the overall memory. For instance, as well as getting a motorcyclist to tell me about the crash we "mock up" a motorbike in the therapy room, so that he is sitting at the same height in the same way as the accident, and then getting him to lie exactly in the same way as he fell, making the same movements. Remember, the memories are not just stored in terms of a sequence of events, like a scientific report, but are stored using similar sense modalities as during the accident. This includes movement, visual-spatial sense, smell, and touch.

Memory recall should be in the present tense. The person should try to recall past events as if they are happening now (e.g. "I am driving down the road", not "I was driving down the road"). This sense of immediacy heightens the emotional impact of the memory.

Memory recall should be in the first person. The person should describe it as seen through their own eyes, as it is happening to them (e.g. "I am trying to steer out of the skid").

Memory recall should not be short but over long periods of time (30–60 minutes). It requires this amount of time to get out the sort of details that are necessary, but also the facing of emotional memories should be prolonged in order to allow habituation to occur. That is, to allow the body enough time for the distressing feelings to calm down somewhat.

Memories should be accessed in as many different formats as possible. This includes writing it down, typing it, reading the written words out loud, having others read out the written words, talking to others about it, reading what was written silently in real time, imagining the events in real time, listening to a tape recording of the account, or expressing it in forms other than words, such as pictures, diagrams, music, art, or dance.

Facing reminders of the trauma. The place where it happened, newspaper accounts, hospital records, police reports, and similar incidents on the TV, movies, radio, or in the conversations of others, should be purposely faced, not avoided.

Recalling the memories while allowing emotional feelings to happen. It is possible for some people to write down or speak out the events while to some extent keeping emotional feelings at bay. Remember that the therapy works not just by facing memories of the event, but also by facing the emotions that are bound up with the memories. Recalling the memories without too much emotion will still help, but for the maximum effect one should allow feelings to come; splashes of tears on the paper is a good sign. For once grammar, spelling, and punctuation are totally unimportant. It is not getting factual or artistic expression onto paper that counts but getting emotional memories out. No one is going to give you a mark out of ten for a good composition.

Having looked at the principles behind facing the memories, now comes the crunch – doing it.

Choose the Right Time to Start

One shouldn't rush into these exercises. It is important to prepare oneself and choose the right time to start. It may be that this approach is not for you – that's fine. It may be that you'd prefer to wait until you find a therapist – that's sensible. As described in the last chapter, it's important to examine one's whole approach to emotions and change aspects of your emotional style in general, before beginning the difficult task of facing the memories of the trauma. Possibly you need more time to get into the right frame of mind. It's important to choose the right time to start because therapy will proceed best if you can have an unbroken run at it. If you are about to change job, house, get married, have a baby, or any other major life change, this is probably not the best time to start. The environment should be relatively stress free (when is it ever totally stress free?), and you will need to have enough time in the next three to six weeks to give this your proper attention.

You need to get as much support as possible from someone who is prepared to listen to you and help. It's important to let those nearest and dearest to you know that they too are in for a bit of a rough ride over the next month or so and to discuss this with them. Once you start to open up, it does tend to flow easier and may be difficult to stop. So count the cost, have everything in place and a clear run ahead of you. In choosing someone to help you, ideally they should be sympathetic and probably not someone who experienced the original trauma with you, otherwise they will be working through issues themselves and may be in less of a position to help you. It would be a good idea in general to open up more to friends and family. At this stage you do not have to open up about the trauma; sharing your thoughts and feelings about little everyday things is a good start and a lot easier than plunging into heavier topics around the trauma. Everything should be done to encourage an open sharing of views even if this runs a bit against the grain.

Getting Access to the Memories

The guiding principle is that the memories of the trauma have not been emotionally processed and the task before you is to fully process them. So, using this guideline, you can be a bit creative and use discretion as to when, how, and to whom – here's a possible schedule of what to do.

Choosing the right means of expression. Writing is probably a good place to start, although you might feel that talking to someone is better for you. At the moment I'm sitting in the garden of our home writing onto notepads with a ballpoint pen. I'm a bit antiquated, but prefer the flow and rhythm of writing by hand. Many people work best on a keyboard into a laptop or PC. Others are most at ease with a dictating machine. There's not a correct "set" way to access the memory – it's what is most natural to you that is important. How will the memories best flow out? Choose a time when you won't be interrupted for about an hour, with the phone off the hook, mobile switched off, and definitely switch off access to emails. It's called creating a space.

Getting into the flow. At first it may be hard to start. "Memory joggers" are needed. Start on the day of the accident or trauma, writing down incidental details – when you got up, how you got ready, what you had to eat, what you wore, what the weather was like... the whole sequence up to the time of the trauma, which you need to go over with the same sort of detail. Some people need a more tangible memory jogger, like a photo of the site of the accident, or the trainers worn at the time, or allowing them to look at or feel the scar received during the accident. What was happening in the news at that time, what time of year it was, what music was popular at that time – these all help to set the scene and may jog the initial memories. As I said, don't worry about the English grammar or getting it absolutely correct – getting the flow is the most important thing. Don't censor it too much, just let it come off the pen or keyboard. Don't expect emotions to come at first – it doesn't matter. What often happens is that the narrative is flowing away without too much emotion and then some little detail, some comment, will be lit up, and – bang – there are the tears. Don't stop. Just keep writing. It's preferable to get it all down in one sitting, but it may be so long that more sittings are needed. If it's just too much, breaks are OK, doing it in stages is OK. It's getting the narrative out that counts.

Remember that you are not a journalist writing a clear, objective account of an accident but the "I" who experiences it subjectively. Try to keep as close to the material as possible by describing it in terms of "I am doing this, I am doing that", and to increase the reality, keep it in the present tense – "I am doing this" rather than "I did this."

Possibly some of the important memories start to emerge at odd times in the day, in which case a notebook is handy to keep a record of these. Flashbacks are, of course, unbidden memories of the accident. If a flashback comes as you are writing, focus on it and try to get down as much detail as you can. Consider it as "essential data" rather than a thing to be feared. Flashbacks, however, can be fixed repetitions of the most frightening seconds of the trauma, unlike piecing together all the surrounding complex of memories that make up the story. It's likely that the new memories that emerge in writing are more diverse than flashbacks – likewise, although dreams may still be frightening in this intense stage of memory recall, they may well start to change as new elements and themes merge into the dreams. Some people find a notebook kept by the bed can be helpful in recalling dreams, although others say they can't remember dreams.

Getting your story down may be a struggle, but when you have got it down, however jumbled it may seem, it's time to give yourself a big pat on the back. It can't have been easy, but if you've made it, well done. It's an important first step in overcoming Post Traumatic Stress Disorder.

Making the most of your narrative. Remember that your story was produced in one mode – written (or typed) words. To get the most out of this account, the modality should be varied.

At first, you could read it silently to yourself, allowing the memories and the emotions to flow as they will. The next stage would be to read the narrative out loud, not to anyone in particular, but to yourself. Up to this stage, the whole exercise may have been completed in silence, so it can sometimes be a surprise at the strength of reaction caused by reading it aloud.

The other person. Talking to another person is a crucial stage in memory recall. Another person is so important because they do not just passively hear the account, but they can add their own reactions to the mix. They can ask questions, react, provide feedback and encouragement, and ground you in realities that may be missing when the account is kept to oneself. As this person may not be a psychological therapist, a good way to structure the "session" is for you to read the account to them, after which a discussion can open up. In this way there's no obligation on them to try to help you retrieve memories – it's all available in the form of your written story.

After the discussion, it may be useful to write down some of the points you discussed together, adding any new observations or thoughts, and in general expanding or rewriting your account.

New ways of making the most of your narrative. So far you may have read your written account silently, out loud to yourself, and spoken to your friend/helper. Now it could be read again silently and thoughtfully, imagining what happened in real time.

Many therapists recommend that you tape record significant sections of the trauma and replay them again and again until you are pretty sick of hearing the same old material. Getting to this incredibly bored stage is one of the triumphs of therapy – we see it as a real step forward. What it really means is that the powerful emotions of horror, fear, and shock have faded, and boredom is about the strongest emotion that can be evoked. Boredom is good in this game!

The other person again. Involving a friend/helper once only is not really sufficient – you need to talk it over with them several times. The first session in which you read out your account was fairly structured; on a second occasion, you might ask them to read out your expanded account. It may seem a bit artificial to you both, but it's likely to cause new reactions. A different modality in presentation may have different emphases and meanings that "reach the parts that other methods can't". Again, this may be followed by open-ended discussion and comments, all of which may increase and cast new light on your memory of the trauma. Keeping a record of this afterwards and changing your narrative is all part of the move towards fuller emotional processing of the memory.

Iterative is the word for this stage. Iterative means taking something, adding to it or changing it in some way into a new version, running it again making more changes, rerunning it and making further changes, and so on. The end product gets closer and closer to the desired end result. This is what is needed. Each time your memory should be getting fuller with new meanings and understandings opening up. By this stage you may be at the fifth or sixth iteration. Also the other person will probably have relaxed and understand your account well, so that your conversations can be freer, less structured, and able to explore various new dimensions. The whole process of communicating your feelings and memories will probably be getting more natural and ordinary even though still difficult.

The narrative should by now be developing into a fuller and fuller account. It's as if it is a complicated jigsaw and the task is to try to put all the pieces together to form the total picture. The early stages of the jigsaw are likely to be the most emotive. As you go over the account, the emotional power of the memories should ultimately decrease. The Post Traumatic symptoms such as flashbacks, nightmares, irritability, and startle should reduce as the memories lose their emotive power, lagging slightly behind progress with the memories.

Visiting the hottest memories. Some parts of the traumatic memory will evoke more distress than others – there may be one or two points of extreme terror. One motorcyclist said the worst memory of all was feeling the crunch as the car hit his legs. For another person, it was the moment at which he thought his car would catch fire. These moments, being the most powerful elements of the emotional memory, require the most work to shift them, so they may need some extra "homework". As memory work proceeds it may be important just to focus on these moments over and over again until they begin to lose their frightening power. At this stage, it will be unnecessary to recall the whole memory sequence once again, only these "hot moments". This is perhaps the time to use a tape recording of your thoughts and memories during the hot moments and listen to it repeatedly.

Exposure to triggers. At the same time as recalling and making sense of the trauma, it is important to start to face all those triggers that may have been avoided. These include:

- Reminders of the trauma on TV, newspapers, movies, conversation, and also official reports such as hospital notes, police reports, photos, or newspaper cuttings.
- Carrying out the activities that were carried out at the time of the trauma. If it was an accident while driving it is time to try to get back to driving again. If it was being a passenger in the accident, it is time to get back as a passenger. Often the person can manage safer approximations to the crash, for example travelling on small roads at quiet times, but finds it extremely difficult to get onto busy motorways or drive at night. In general the closer the person gets to the type of accident the more anxiety they will feel.
- Seeing people who remind them of the assailant, with similar physical appearance and mannerisms, for instance avoiding all bald men because the attacker was bald.
- Going to the place where the trauma happened, or seeing reminders of it, such as the clothes worn, or the type of car driven (as long as this is physically safe).
- Sometimes triggers come in the form of what was felt at the time – pain in the limb that was shattered in the accident might trigger reminders of it. Emotions felt at the time of the accident, such as panic, may likewise trigger memories.

- Sometimes people cannot look at parts of the body injured in an accident. Claire (see Chapter 4) decided to wear long-sleeved dresses not just to cover the burns on her arms from the view of others but so she did not have to see her own arm. When she showered in the morning she closed her eyes to avoid seeing her arm. Facing these triggers would mean looking at the injured area for long enough for the strong emotions to subside.

- Sometimes the impact of the trauma seems to spread very widely so that almost any little reminder can trigger a reaction. In Chapter 1, Jason did not want to go out because even the pavement, usually regarded as a place of safety, was now seen as dangerous. Everywhere outside seemed dangerous. Where crimes or rapes occur inside one's own home, the sanctity and security of one's most trusted haven can be shattered. In cases like this, multiple things must be faced and tolerated; the work is long and hard.

Demolishing avoidance clutter. With all these triggers – stimuli that have been avoided through fear of the emotional reaction – it is now necessary to face them again. All sorts of avoidance reactions can be built up over time, making the person feel quite imprisoned. Therapy involves dismantling the clutter of avoidance. Sometimes people can do these in a "one-off" confrontation, but others have to take the "softly softly" approach. One man I saw for a motorbike accident shivered and shook even when looking at what before had been his beloved bike and avoided going near his garage. For him, dismantling the avoidance involved a slow sequence of looking at his bike from afar, then a week later standing right next to it, and after that sitting on it, sitting on it with the engine on, riding down the path, riding up the back lane, riding on minor roads at quiet times, riding at busier times, with the finale, riding his bike down the motorway at rush hour. As he successfully mastered each stage, and stuck with it long enough for the anxiety to subside, he was able to take on the next stage. Often this means facing things for 35–50 minutes, not just taking a quick look.

If the person has stopped carrying out activities such as driving, or socializing with others over quite a period of time, this may have built into a behavioural habit that may require more time and a more intensive push to overcome. In a way the problem has moved from an avoidance of feeling emotions to a fixed pattern of behaviour.

From Boredom Point to Freedom Point

Most of this therapy is based on repetition – repetition to the point at which it is no longer distressing, moving, if you like, towards the boredom point. For some people this is quicker than for others, but if therapy is fairly intense the eye of the storm can be three weeks long. Going over the narrative daily will bring quicker progress than weekly. Longer sessions of facing what was feared (30–60 minutes) are usually better. Really intensive work cuts down the total time, but may not be possible or may just be too emotionally demanding.

Everyone needs to find their own pace. It will not be comfortable. Whatever pace is chosen, however, it is best to move closer towards two or three sessions a week, rather than once a week.

Sometimes after a really intensive "push" over a few weeks, a holiday from the memories is a good thing. The break is often useful and gives new perspective. It is necessary to decide the length of the holiday in advance, starting again as planned.

Try to tune in to your own emotional intuition about the pace of therapy and listen to the advice of those close to you. If you hit problems during the therapy talk to those closest to you and seek professional advice if necessary. Sometimes things may not be working out as expected. You can't go on forever if something is not working. There may come a point when it is wiser to stop the battle and pull back rather than to keep persisting without results. Recognizing when to concede could be important.

If you have carried out the preliminary general work described in Chapter 12, and have successfully processed the traumatic memories as described in this chapter, not only should PTSD symptoms be improving but there should also be a noticeable improvement in your communication and relationship with those who are closest to you. You should notice the difference and they should too.

Coping with Setbacks

In recovering from PTSD, the ability to cope with setbacks is crucial. It can make the difference between a successful recovery and abandoning therapy. The first thing to get fixed in the mind is that setbacks are normal and are to be expected. Whether being seen by a therapist or carrying out self-therapy, there will be setbacks and disappointments. Progress in therapy is definitely not even. Figure 3 (below) shows the typical progress of what happens during a course of therapy. The downward line shows progress over a six to nine month period. As we move from week to week and session to session, there are many ups and downs. This is normal. Overall, over a period of several months, there is movement towards recovery, but from week to week it will vary. Take point A. There seems to be an amazingly quick recovery, "Great, I'm nearly over it, no more flashbacks or nightmares for me." Then we hit point B: "Oh no, three flashbacks today. I'm back to square one. What's the point? Therapy is not working." Well no, you're not back to square one; you've slipped a little in the short term, but looked at from a long term perspective, there is progress. Actually, really rapid progress can be a problem because it sets too high a standard for when progress is slower.

There may still be occasional flashbacks even after treatment has finished, especially if you have been going through a more stressful time than usual, or are run down, overworked, or physically unwell. The whole problem has not returned, it's just a blip, and by using what was successful before you can usually get over it quite quickly.

Figure 3. The course of therapy

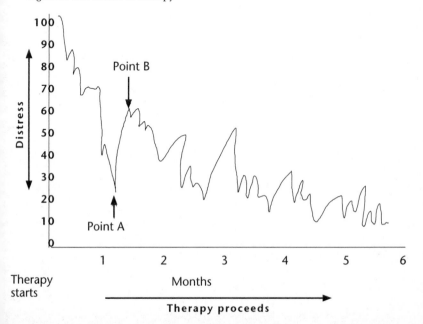

The Journey Onwards

Chapter 15

Stumbling Blocks

Most of the case histories discussed so far have explored what Post Traumatic Stress is, its psychological components, and how therapy works. Like any condition, it is not always straightforward; complexities, elaborations, and exceptions arise. Think of PTSD as something like a language, obeying a set of core grammatical rules, but also with some more superficial irregularities and exceptions. It is probably best not to think of English, however, where exceptions seem to be roughly equivalent to the basic rules. In this section I would like to explain some of the main complications that hold therapy back, before moving on to what can take the therapy forward even further.

The self-help programme described in Section IV is an excellent therapy approach for overcoming the core Post Traumatic Stress condition and covers the whole range of PTSD symptoms. Sometimes, however, it is not so much PTSD symptoms but other issues flowing from the trauma that can stall the therapy. Let's consider five major stumbling blocks:

1. **Disability resulting from the trauma.** If we lose the use of any function that we have come to rely on – sight, hearing, being able to run – it can be devastating. Even a relatively small loss, such as not being able to bend a knee as well as before, can have many repercussions on our exercise levels, or the speed at which we can move around, which may result in becoming overweight. So, imagine the loss of both legs in a motorbike accident. This happened to Connor, a young man in an unexpected motorbike accident in which he was left unable to walk properly. Post Traumatic Stress symptoms were

distressing him greatly, but also a range of other losses had devastated his life. These included: loss of his chosen career (physiotherapy); loss of his girlfriend; being unable to continue his active pursuit of sports; financial loss and dependency on the state; repeated surgery; and constant pain that acted as a trigger for flashbacks and deprived him of sleep. It was these other consequences of the trauma that made it so difficult for Connor to complete his course of Emotional Processing Therapy. In a way, Connor needed to overcome and recover from every single area of loss in his life. Yes, he was troubled by flashbacks and nightmares, but in the context of all his losses, the effective therapy of PTSD symptoms was only part of his recovery.

2. **Secondary traumas resulting from the original trauma.** Sometimes the original trauma leads to a series of subsequent traumas. For Vivian, when the surgeon told her, "I'm afraid I have to tell you it's a cancerous lump in your breast," this constituted the focal trauma, setting off nightmares and flashbacks. But a series of other traumas followed – chemotherapy, not being able to get the needles in for the infusion, sudden loss of her hair, thrombosis as a side effect of her medication, being "abandoned" in Casualty while she was unable to breathe, and surgical removal of her breast. Also, these mini-traumas compounded the original trauma of hearing the cancer diagnosis. Therapy involved thinking about and working through every single trauma as well as trying to address the massive changes to her everyday life.

3. **Anger towards the person who caused the trauma.** Although the person may be able to face the memories of the trauma, they sometimes get stuck when it comes to thinking about the person who caused the trauma. Connor, who had lost so much when a car that was travelling down the wrong side of the road hit his motorbike head on, had to face something else. In court, the eighteen-year-old driver did not apologize, blamed Connor, showed no remorse, and through a clever legal team escaped with only six points on his licence. "I went blank," said Connor. "There was no relief. It was just a slap on the wrist. I was brought up to be honest. He lied and didn't accept responsibility for wrecking my life. He said

he saw no one and it wasn't his fault. I would have said sorry out of respect for another human being, but he was matter of fact and didn't care. He hasn't written. There's no justice in the world." Understandably Connor was angry – angry with the defence lawyers, the legal system, but most of all angry with the eighteen-year-old driver. A single apology, a sign of remorse, a small attempt at restitution, or even recognition of the harm he had done to Connor's life would have been enough to calm Connor's rage. The response of the driver was none of these.

Such an injustice can enrage sufferers to the extent that the anger becomes all-pervasive. Occasionally therapy is proceeding well as more and more traumatic memories unfold, and then when it comes to thinking about the perpetrator of the trauma, the anger can be so intense and prolonged that Emotional Processing Therapy is put on hold until the anger is dealt with. Sometimes the person cannot overcome their anger and bitterness, and therapy permanently stalls. Fortunately Connor placed a high premium on forgiveness and had always regarded bitterness as destructive to his own mental health, so he worked really hard at "forgiving the unforgivable". So for him, at least, anger did not significantly overtake therapy. For others it can.

4. Guilt and shame. In a way what happens here is similar to the case of anger: an overwhelmingly powerful emotion can put the brake on Emotional Processing Therapy. If a motorist has run over a child in a car accident he may be racked with guilt as well as suffering from Post Traumatic Stress symptoms. The guilt is usually present from the start of therapy but could emerge as a more significant barrier to progress at a later stage. The guilt may be legitimate (he was drunk while driving) or unjustified (the child ran out while he was driving carefully within the speed limit). The driver might feel guilty for not doing enough to avert the accident. Often there is a range of uncertainties that make it difficult to establish culpability. The press, the law, or other people may accuse justifiably or not. Whether the guilt is legitimate or unjustified makes no difference to the psychological impact on the person. If they believe it, it will have an impact on them.

A type of guilt reported by those who have been sexually abused as children is that they feel somehow responsible for "enticing" the abuser. This often follows a certain type of brainwashing by the abuser that they were too provocative and "made me do it". An adult can easily intellectually manipulate a six-year-old. Usually the whole affair is clouded in secrecy, with the child being bullied into never telling anyone else. Guilt can also follow if any pleasurable sensations were felt by the abused. So, guilt and shame, like anger, might hinder therapy for PTSD symptoms, until it has been addressed, understood, and effectively worked through.

5. **A court case or financial settlement that has not been completed**, in other words "incomplete resolution". It has been long recognized in financial-legal settings that it is hard for patients to totally let go of psychological symptoms (whether consciously or unconsciously) until their case has been fully resolved. To be totally symptom-free almost seems emotionally to represent, "Well, there is no need to continue with the settlement." It is often observed by patients themselves and by others that their symptoms get markedly better after (favourable) compensation. This has led to draconian legislation in the past; the German "Reichversicherungs Ordnung" of 1926 regarded traumatic conditions as "compensation neurosis", and ensured that such disability was no longer to be compensated.[1] This overly harsh interpretation mistakenly regarded compensation as the cause of PTSD rather than a complicating factor in the course of the condition. Many PTSD sufferers are involved in litigation of one sort or another, and it is very often their experience that the protracted settlement, haggling, and counter accusations from the defendant's solicitors hang like a pall over their lives and can seriously interfere with the effectiveness of therapy.

I have chosen one particular case history of a patient that illustrates in more depth how these different issues of disability, anger, guilt, shame, and incomplete resolution interplay with Emotional Processing Therapy, prolonging PTSD symptoms. It is the case of Jules, a top-level businessman whose successful career was a defining attribute of his persona. It wasn't so much the personal trauma in his life, but more the prolonged hospital treatment and his residual disabilities that rocked him to the core. The case of Max, presented in Chapter 11, was a straightforward example of successful therapy – it was chosen to be a clear illustration of how Emotional Processing Therapy works. The case of Jules, on the other hand, was chosen to show the complications involved.

Chapter 16

The Deal

Jules was what you might call a "self-made man". After gaining his degree in business and advertising he joined a succession of firms which, through his exceptional drive and business acumen, took him to marketing vice-president position of a major manufacturing company by the age of thirty-five. For two years he had been working flat out, brokering his own company's takeover of another, which would make them a major player in their market. The day of the ultimate "deal" joining the two companies was fast approaching and Jules had everything prepared, all loopholes covered. He described himself as intense, competitive, able to work at speed, incredibly decisive, and actually a bit arrogant, that is, before the trauma. He was the man who always got things done; his colleagues were so sure of his ability to achieve his goals that the takeover became something of a fact of life rather than a hope for the future. They all expected him to clinch the ultimate big one, the company's expansion. In his home life, it was a similar story; his goals were to reach the highest level of personal development. He regularly carried out a range of sports, particularly weights, kept to a strict diet, and had an active social life, that is, as long as it didn't interfere with his pursuit of "the deal". He did say he felt that he never needed other people. He enjoyed their company but felt pretty self-sufficient. His enthusiasm and optimism made him popular with others. He moved around the world at quite a speed, particularly the US, where the other company was based. Unfortunately there was a cost to his dynamism. His first two marriages had broken up, his second wife having left him "because of his commitment to work rather than his commitment to me". He told me that he felt completely in control of his life – "You make your own destiny" was the way he put it.

The previous year he had met Janie and they had bought a beautiful rural property on the Isle of Wight.

So, we come to the week of "the deal". His life, as he said, was coming to a "focal point". His work had become more hectic as he brought everything together, with many trips to the Far East and the States.

In the run up to the deal, he enjoyed an evening meal at a West End restaurant with Andrew, the director working for him. He returned to sleep at his London flat but woke early in the morning in excruciating pain. It seemed to be unrelenting and he just couldn't shift it. Normally he would "tough out" ailments but it was so bad he rang Janie and asked her to come and take him home. She arrived that afternoon. On the journey home he started to vomit, and so she took him to the Accident and Emergency Department in a hospital on the way back to the Isle of Wight. He was examined, told it was food poisoning, and sent away with painkillers. But, back at home the painkillers had no effect. He felt extremely weak and was tossing and turning with pain in his stomach. "I've never felt pain like that before," he said. He began to have blood in his urine, for which a locum doctor prescribed antibiotics. Jules continued to deteriorate. By the time everyone realized how serious his condition was – his stomach had swollen and his legs were purple – the delay in getting him airlifted to Southampton General Hospital was nearly fatal. By this time his appendix had burst, with peritonitis and other complications. After a series of operations he was transferred to ITU (Intensive Therapies Unit), and his family were told he was unlikely to survive more than a few days. He was unconscious for ten days, waking up in ITU, where he was semi-conscious for many days. He stayed in ITU for three and a half weeks altogether, followed by a further three months in hospital. Needless to say, "the deal" was never closed.

On the Scrap Heap

When I first saw Jules for an assessment to establish whether a course of Cognitive Behaviour Therapy would help him, it was nearly three years after his appendicitis. He had taken a year to recover physically from the aftermath of appendicitis and had gone back to work in the same firm as marketing director, which was far less pressurized and was substantially less well paid. He did not have the drive and energy he had had before and mourned the loss of his "intensity". He wished he could get his competitive edge back, but could not push himself in the same way. He said his new job was more person-oriented, which he saw as a softer option – he was coping well but missed the drive towards deadlines and goals as previously. He was self-conscious about his looks; he had lost a lot of muscle tone while lying in his hospital bed, and had gained weight. Although he had dieted and lost weight when first leaving hospital, he was prone to comfort eat now. He had a distended stomach, with a large abdominal scar, and a tracheotomy scar in his throat, which mildly affected his speech. He was sure he could never be taken on as a chief executive officer now because he didn't look the part of a dynamic director. He was "on the scrap heap", as he said. His sense of being a strong male in charge of his destiny had been eroded. He said, "This sort of thing shatters the illusion that you have power over your own destiny. It is hard to accept that you are vulnerable physically, emotionally, and mentally." He said he could give a convincing imitation of a director in full control of his department, but he felt it was an act, and rather an effort to keep up this drive for long periods. Actually in the session he was open, friendly, and sharp witted and appeared to be natural enough. The erosion of his persona was uppermost in his mind when he talked to me on this first occasion, but he was also troubled by significant Post Traumatic Stress symptoms and knew that it was this that was the primary target for treatment.

But the more Jules told me about what had happened, the less certain I became about what was actually the trauma. If you take flashbacks and nightmares to be an accurate indicator of what was most traumatic, they revolved around his time in hospital; dreams of drowning as he was being turned in his hospital bed, and the confusing bleeps, warning sounds, and noise of an intensive therapies unit.

The memories of his appendicitis got vaguer the closer he got to losing consciousness some time before it burst. He remembered the pain and snippets of conversation between Janie and the doctor, of Janie crying when she had to leave for work, and waiting for the ambulance men to arrive. He had felt there was something seriously wrong with him and, unusually for him, he experienced a feeling of fear, fear that he would die a painful death. He couldn't remember the paramedics arriving but did remember voices of real concern as he was taken from the ambulance to the helicopter, which made him panic. He thought he had been delirious, and the whole experience was vague, patchy, and more characterized by sensations than events. Flashbacks could be set off by smells and bodily movements rather than visual pictures of a series of events.

In the Intensive Therapies Unit, Jules lay in bed almost totally paralysed. He couldn't speak, move, breathe, feed himself, or urinate, so he was attached to an artificial breathing machine with a tracheotomy line fitted directly into his windpipe, and a range of other devices that took over his life functions. He was heavily sedated with painkillers and other medications.

Significant memories of his hospital treatment revolved around regaining consciousness. He said, "The two and a half weeks of unconsciousness really blew me. They kept me in forced unconsciousness for that time. I woke up with all this going on around me. I didn't know who they were or what was going on. I couldn't understand why people were putting a bag over my face. I couldn't understand why I couldn't move. You have no control over your life at all. Strange faces I couldn't communicate with. I was isolated from the rest of the world. I can't put memories in chronological order – they are fuzzy memories." He mentioned at this stage that there were hospital notes, and the family and nurses had kept a diary for him and there were many get-well cards, but he was unable to look at or read them.

"Those early stages in ITU seemed to be a nightmare of waking up, a sense of panic that I didn't know where I was, and people's faces were very close. It was a fear of the unknown. Why was I there? What is going to happen? I was lost in limbo, drifting between consciousness and unconsciousness."

Jules tried to avoid reminders of his trauma. He avoided hospital if possible or television scenes reminiscent in any way of hospitals or illness. Stomach pains or any medical issues were a great worry. He could not go to the dentist because of an extreme reaction to the sound of the suction device, which resembled the suction of mucous from his tracheotomy tube, which was a regular feature in ITU. He had lost interest in many former pursuits and did not like to go out or socialize much. His sexual libido was much reduced. Janie felt he had changed from an extrovert to an introvert. He was more irritable, but she had been very patient and understanding.

Planning Therapy

I agreed to see Jules regularly for a course of twelve sessions of psychological therapy initially. It later transpired that seven more sessions were needed because of the complexity of his case. From the point of view of Emotional Processing Therapy, the problem seemed to be the lack of a clear memory of events. The memories were vague and out of sequence. However, although the visual narrative was patchy, he did have many memories of a kinaesthetic kind. For instance, "A smell may trigger a memory snapshot that stops me in my tracks – the degrading feeling of being put in a chair and hoisted upwards to attend my personal care." Therapy might be more a case of helping to retrieve and face lost and vague memories rather than facing consciously suppressed memories.

In our therapy sessions it was clear I was dealing with a businessman. I usually began the sessions by offering him tea or coffee, leaving the therapy office for a couple of minutes while I prepared his coffee. Invariably when I returned he had read and answered a few emails on his blackberry – no second was to be wasted – and this was him in his "less intense" mode! Jules imposed his own control on the sessions – not in any inappropriate or bossy way – it was just that he was aware of his goals, formed a clear agenda and, as sessions progressed, he organized and expanded on his homework exercises and seemed to know just where he was going. When it became clear to him that we needed to go through the entire four months of his stay in hospital in detail, he "blocked" his therapy into six distinct stages. We worked away at each stage until he had recalled the relevant memories and got everything in place, and then we moved on to the next stage.

His stages were:

1. the ruptured appendix

2. the slow regaining of consciousness in ITU

3. his attempts to understand what had happened to him

4. having understood what was happening around him, not having any control over it

5. his transfer off ITU to other wards as he regained physical functions

6. regaining the ability to communicate and regain control of his life.

From High Control to No Control

While he had gone over the appendicitis a few times with his solicitor and partner, he had not thought in much detail about his stay in hospital, which engendered so many fears. Going into the details seemed to clarify his thinking, bring to light lost memories, and generally help him get mental control back over his chaotic experiences. In his memory the appendicitis seemed disjointed from all his other memories. In filling in the Emotional Processing Scale in our first session the dissociation score was high, including "my emotions felt blunt/dull", "my feelings did not seem to belong to me", and "there seemed to be a big blank in my feelings", suggesting the confused and half-remembered memories were partly cut off from his consciousness. As he recovered these memories, his sense of detachment was replaced by a more cohesive feeling.

In discussing his problems of regaining consciousness he distinguished the waking up, associated with feelings of panic and confusion, with fear of going to sleep. He mentioned being constantly in darkness, with the sensation of drifting off to sleep feeling like being sucked into darkness. He feared the darkness and being permanently alone. He felt that the fear of unconsciousness differed in some way from the fear of death. He mentioned the comfort of being able to see the nurse's station, although he couldn't see below his own chest. He remembered that the patient next to him died, which had quite an impact on him and on the nursing staff.

There was much detailed discussion around the mechanics of having all his life functions controlled by others. He talked of the regular suction in the tracheotomy tube – "There was a lot of crap coming off my chest which needed to be sucked up." If the nurse talked him through this, he felt more secure. His mouth was very dry, and they gave him some "pink stuff", which tasted disgusting. If something got stuck in his throat he panicked, but was unable to communicate this to anyone, nor was he able to look round and understand what was happening. He described a different phase of his recuperation when the ventilator was switched off. He panicked because he couldn't breathe, and again, he couldn't communicate this. Very often we returned to the horror of being completely at the mercy of nurses, and having no control of breathing, swallowing, and movement. For Jules, control of his own life was extremely important, and here he was stripped of even the most basic types of control. As he said, "I was operating at the level of basic instincts."

Adding to the confusion of the experience was the fact that Jules was heavily medicated throughout. In one session he remembered something quite extraordinary. At night-time he regularly saw two figures outside the window of the ward. The taller figure wore a top hat like Abraham Lincoln. He was frightened of them and cried but could not move. If he took his eyes off them or fell asleep, he thought they might come and get him. "It became a strong match. You won't get me. They couldn't get through the window while I was awake." He felt that as long as he stayed awake they were unable to "get him" and he struggled hard not to sleep. He managed to successfully keep them at bay. "They disappeared when the sun came up."

It would be tempting simply to call this a hallucination caused by his heavy dose of medication, yet having explained that he was operating in pre-logical mode, where symbolism, like the symbolism of dreams, predominates, we were able to explore possible meanings. After a short while he was able to identify that the taller figure was like the grim reaper – "death and his side-kick were constantly watching me, waiting to get me". They were the epitome of evil. He felt his battle with them represented an extremely stubborn streak in him to win the battle and not let go. In a way he was acting out his own stubborn struggle to stay alive. By sheer grit and determination he feels that he hung on.

Loss of My Private Shield

Jules started to share his feelings on the toilet cleaning routine. Having no control over his bladder and bowels involved nurses cleaning his excreta, washing him, and at various times fitting and removing a catheter. "I experienced degradation in myself as a person and a man. I felt totally vulnerable. My dignity was lost, lying in my own excreta. A part of me was disgusted. The majority of the nurses who cleaned me were female, often young, making me feel weak and incapable. I've never been in that situation before." He felt it was a process of emasculation, "profoundly affecting my intimacy and sex life. Lying there with an open wound, on public display – was beyond sex. Everybody *can* see inside of me." He did not say "everybody *could* see inside of me", in the past tense, but "everybody *can* see inside of me", in the present tense, as if he were actually reliving the sense of being on public display. Even now, three years later, he was having problems with his libido despite a very close and loving relationship with his partner. "My weakness is open to all." I asked what showing weakness meant to him. "In previous intimate relationships I was able to share weakness. I *chose* to show weakness and *chose* when I was in charge, in control."

I was puzzled as to how he had tolerated his short spell in the army as a young man if he needed to be in control all the time, and quizzed him on this. "If you have respect for your sergeant, it was OK to take orders. It was hard to take orders if I didn't respect them but I wasn't out of control. I was choosing to put myself under them. It was my personal choice to go into the army... not to have personal choice is to remove the strength from a person – remove their humanness."

It was clearer to me now that the trauma of those early days of recovery impinged on what the psychologist George Kelly called a "core construct".[1] For Jules, being in control was a central part of his way of being, almost a philosophy of life, and it wasn't hard to see how the experience had shaken him so deeply.

"The Naughty Boy"

Even though Jules could hardly move at this stage he tried to gain some control over his life. He confessed that on one occasion when he was taken for an MRI scan and turned rather painfully he purposely pulled out his tracheotomy tube. But it was not just trying to get control – he was desperately trying to communicate. He would use facial expressions to indicate what he wanted, which the nurses found amusing, much to his satisfaction. He tried to be jokey, "forever playing practical jokes on people in a slapstick way". He enjoyed female company and flirted with the nurses. "How did you get your sense of control back?" I asked.

"It came back with physical movement. Speech was denied me. When I started to move my arms I could make a fuss with anyone. I could take control back. You don't need much physical movement to make it awkward and pull out tubes. I was aggressive at first, trying to win back control, but I didn't need to be. Sometimes I could be in control by being tearful or by being polite. As I progressed, my humour came back, and then I used to make jokes about being indignant. It made me feel better, in control."

Jules thought his transfer off ITU was significant and felt that this was entering into a new stage of therapy. It included eating by himself, starting to speak again, and learning to walk. The process of removing his tracheotomy tube and inserting a "speaking valve" was difficult, and he hated using the speaking valve, although he did realize that "speaking meant taking control back". "It was probably a good thing that they told me I'd never be able to walk properly. It gave me the determination to prove they were wrong." In his battle to get walking he had caught a glimpse of himself in a mirror and was frightened by the weak person he saw, with no muscle definition. He did get back to full mobility and eventually to jogging again, although he couldn't push himself to the same level he had previously.

Post Traumatic Growth

One of Jules' "homework" assignments had been to read the get-well cards and letters he had been sent. He had previously not looked at a single card because he "chose not to let the emotions come to the surface". On reflection the extended time I had spent with Jules at the start of therapy explaining the need to face emotions ensured that when he did, it was his decision. If we had started too soon and I forced him to feel emotions he didn't want to, it might have met with resistance. When Jules came to the therapy session the following week he was "bowled over" by the number of well-wishers, cards, and the kind thoughts and prayers of so many people. He described how Janie's support throughout had been a source of strength and encouragement for him, and he had been surprised at the level of continued care and support from his family; he thought that after an initial visit they might lose interest. Although he had been a "naughty boy" with the nursing staff he was full of admiration for their determined care too. Later, he read the daily log kept by Janie and the nursing staff showing so many personal moments of intimacy and care.

Towards the end of therapy I asked what positive benefits had come from the whole experience, how he had grown personally. He actually answered with a negative: "If I had not been taken out of the loop for six months – if I had seen the deal through – it would have had an impact on my career. The choice was taken away from me." He told me that he had been a goal-directed person, but now, he said in a wistful tone, he was much more person-centred. I asked if there might be a positive element in this. I think he could only focus on his loss at this time, although it was clear to me that he was doing rather well in his more "person-centred" job, that Janie was finding him easier to live with, and well, couldn't it just be that other people warmed to him more? He could half see this; I suspect that when he has achieved a little more at work, and let the many revelations he had made settle down a bit, he may start to appreciate more that humanity is about personal closeness as well as personal control. Certainly Jules had been extremely open with me – he had not really held anything back, and despite being the driven businessman actually related to me in a warm and human way.

His emotions, previously described in terms of being somewhat disjointed from his everyday experience, of feeling blank or dull, and as if they did not belong to him, now had the sense of central integration within himself. His dissociation score on the full Emotional Processing Scale had declined from 51 per cent (seriously high) to 15 per cent (normal). His scores on suppression of emotion, avoidance of emotion, and degree of unprocessed emotional material had likewise shown substantial improvement from dysfunctional to normal levels. His anxiety symptoms were now scoring at normal levels, and his self-esteem scores had improved. I suppose one of the most important factors, his level of PTSD symptomatology, as indicated by the Davidson Trauma questionnaire (see Chapter 11) given on three separate occasions during the therapy, moved from ninety-two to thirty-four, then to eleven. What this represents is a move from being nearly at the maximum score for PTSD symptoms at the start, to a normal healthy level of functioning at the end. Jules, for whom the issue of controlling his life was so important, had undoubtedly been helped by describing and understanding in detail what had happened. It provided a sense of mental mastery and control over thoughts and feelings that were previously chaotic. Phew! It wasn't simple; it wasn't all about PTSD symptoms; it wasn't all about emotions either. Everything was embedded in the wider context of his personal values and what life meant to him.

Chapter 17

Sweet or Deadly Oblivion?

At 8.50 a.m. on 7 July 2005, three bombs exploded within fifty seconds of each other on three London Underground trains. At that time in the morning the trains were packed with commuters and the carnage was appalling. Fifty-six people died, including the suicide bombers, and 700 people were injured. In the Piccadilly Line tunnel Gill Hicks was in carriage 346, where one of the bombs exploded. The train was deep inside the tunnel, and it took the emergency services nearly an hour to reach her. She lost five pints of blood and her heart stopped beating twice. She later recalled that as she lay amongst the darkness and the smoke, trying to understand what was happening, she felt death was very close. "I was offered a choice – the voice of life was urging me to remember what was important about being alive. I had had a row with my boyfriend the night before but then I just wanted to get back to Joe. There was a strange objective strength that was trying to disconnect me from getting panicky." A TV documentary, *The Miracle of Carriage 346*,[1, 2] documents her survival. Gill lost both of her legs in the bombing but surprisingly in the documentary didn't appear at all bitter or regretful. She talked of the realization of how much her relationship with Joe meant to her, and of her determination to walk again before they married. She described all the hard work of rehabilitation to reach her wedding, and walking down the aisle on her prosthetic legs. "The place was absolutely filled. It finished off the whole church. They were all blubbing. I walked well." She went on to establish a charity aimed at working for world peace. She said, "You don't know your strength until you are faced with something like this." Other survivors interviewed for the documentary also spoke of positive personal benefits after the disaster, such as a greater closeness to their family, or a changed perspective on life, which speaks of a different side of the coin to the debilitating, negative symptoms of Post Traumatic Stress.

Post Traumatic Growth

These positive reactions are, it seems, not uncommon. "We have found that reports of growth experiences in the aftermath of traumatic events far outnumber reports of psychiatric disorders." This is the astonishing claim of psychologists Richard Tedeschi and Lawrence Calhoun of the University of North Carolina,[3] who have been studying Post Traumatic Growth over a twenty-year period.[4] Through this research and interview studies by others,[5] six positive types of growth have been regularly found:

1. **Developing a sense of personal strength.** This was one of the things reported by Gill Hicks. Tedeschi and Calhoun point to a paradox in which individuals report an increased sense of vulnerability consistent with the suffering they have been unable to prevent, yet also an increased feeling of their own capacity to survive and prevail. "I am more vulnerable, yet stronger." Objectively speaking we might expect Jules, described in the previous chapter, to report this – by his own strength of will he had dragged himself out of a vegetative state to full functioning, yet he was also displaying a sensitivity to others, not present before his appendicitis. But he did not feel it this way. He did not perceive it as "growth", rather as an obstacle to the return of his former dynamic self.

2. **A greater appreciation of life.** Sometimes there is a greater appreciation of the ordinary things in life, often with a re-alignment of priorities. One man spoke of the pace of his previously hectic, work-driven life; he had slowed down a lot, spent much more time with his son, and realized the importance of "taking time to smell the roses".

3. **Getting closer to other people**, particularly family. There is often a realization that relationships are more important than previously thought. Tedeschi and Calhoun point out that the need for the person to talk about and share the

traumatic event can send close relationships one of two ways. Some relationships "pass the test", often bringing partners and family closer together. Some relationships don't stand the strain, bringing disharmony and breakdown. Sometimes survivors get more comfortable with intimacy. One lady described, in a reluctant sort of way, how previously she was "like an island ... but that I had to accept help from other people, and that was really hard for me to do. So now I am a bit more open to that."

4. Greater self-understanding. In struggling to come to terms with the trauma and its effect on them, people learn a lot about themselves. Often people feel changed in some way. In PTSD, the person often feels profoundly changed for the worse, but it can work the other way. One lady said, "I can't see my life without it now. It is very character building, and I like the person I am now... I wouldn't want to be another person."

5. Spiritual development. Traumatic events often throw open fundamental existential questions about death and the purpose of life. Previous assumptions about life may be shattered for many trauma survivors, ushering in a period of intense questioning of their beliefs. This grappling with spiritual issues takes place not in the relaxed atmosphere of everyday life, or in an abstract, intellectual way, but is forged in the fire of powerful experience. For some there will be a deepening of faith, but for others a loss of faith. William Paul Young's novel *The Shack*[6] is a wonderful example of someone wrestling with difficult issues until a spiritual transformation is reached. The book describes the journey taken by Mack, a bitter and traumatized father of a young daughter who had been abducted and murdered by a child abuser. It is a moving account of how he finds a higher perspective and meaning for what appears to be irreconcilable tragedy. Ultimately, he can never forget what happened but finds a transforming resolution for his distress. The struggle with these spiritual issues, often intensely painful, can lead to a sense of experiencing life at a deeper level of awareness. One woman put it like this: "It feels good at a soul level... I guess I look deeper at things, from less of a 'me' perspective."

6. Opening up of new possibilities. In Chapter 11, Max, who had fallen during his work as a window cleaner, was looking forward to a change in direction to plumbing, but only after successfully overcoming the most severe symptoms of Post Traumatic Stress. Others may change direction, or perspective in life, without first having to go through a period of psychological therapy.

Tedeschi and Calhoun make the important point that it is not a question of either Post Traumatic Stress or Post Traumatic Growth. "Instead, continuing personal distress and growth often co-exist."[7] Growth is not an inevitable consequence of trauma; for some the trauma seems to be only destructive. But the promising thing is that growth is possible. It's rather like the pearl, a thing of beauty, formed over a long process from the irritation of a speck of grit. Likewise, Post Traumatic Growth emerges not directly from the trauma itself, but from the person's struggle to cope with the aftermath of the trauma.

Eternal Sunshine of the Spotless Mind

While this speaks of growth through adversity, there is an entirely different solution on the horizon: remove the adversity. I don't mean remove the adversity in the sense of making what has happened, not happen. This would be the earnest wish of many PTSD sufferers, but unfortunately reality cannot be changed like that. What I am talking about comes close, though. It's not removing the traumatic event; it's removing the *memory* of the traumatic event. This is the stuff of films such as *Eternal Sunshine of the Spotless Mind*, in which Jim Carrey plays a character who has an unhappy love affair erased from his memory, or *Paycheck*, in which Ben Affleck's character agrees to carry out top secret work for his company and then have his memory erased. The science hasn't quite got to the point the movies have, but neuroscience institutes, pharmaceutical companies, and medical and psychology departments are reaching towards the development of "forget" substances that can be administered after a trauma to interfere with the storage and recall of traumatic memories.

One distressing type of trauma sometimes reported by patients after surgery is being conscious at the time of surgery but not able to move in order to inform the surgeons, resulting in much pain and distress. "Pre-medicants" of the benzodiazepine class, such as midazolam and flunitrazepam, are administered before some operations so that any traumatic memories of the operation are not properly stored and recalled. Whether this is to reduce distress or to reduce litigation, I'm not sure. But as with many drugs, it can be misused. Flunitrazepam, otherwise known as Rohypnol, is the drug often referred to as the "date rape drug". Its ability to cause semi-consciousness and memory block-outs means that in the wrong hands it is used to spike drinks so that the victim can be raped but not remember enough to bring a cogent police case against the rapist. As with other illicit drugs, it is advertised on the Internet as "order on-line, easy/fast. No prescription required".

There are other "pre-forget" drugs available with different chemical reactions, such as anti-depressants like tryptanol, beta-adrenoceptor blocking drugs like Inderal, and anaesthetic drugs such as propofol or scopolamine. The uses range from giving it to emergency rescue workers before they go to clean up body parts from a plane crash, to offering it to prisoners about to be executed. What the researchers are edging towards is a "post-forget" substance, one that can be administered after a trauma to erase or block the memory of the traumatic event, while hopefully leaving more benign memories untouched.

Dr Todd Sacktor leads a neuroscience team at the SUNY Downstate Medical Center, Brooklyn, investigating how certain proteins and molecules can disrupt and undo traumatic memories using mice as prototypes for understanding human biochemistry.[8] His team have identified a specific molecule, PKMzeta, which, if blocked, seems to completely eradicate the memories of painful electric shocks, in mice at least. The point is that there are many research centres throughout the world engaged in this same endeavour, some working at a biochemical level as this group does, others using brain scans in humans to identify the effect of substances on different regions of the brain, and others using psychological memory tasks to identify the impact of drugs. It is probably not far off the time when a pharmaceutical company will market a drug aimed at blocking the memory of a trauma in order to prevent the development of Post Traumatic Stress Disorder. Is this the ultimate answer to PTSD?

It does sound appealing but, to spoil the dream, most drugs in psychiatry have a partial effect, or benefit some individuals but not others. And then, of course, many drugs carry a risk of side effects.

Prozac, for instance, was marketed as a "happiness" drug; so effective it could be used by healthy people to improve the quality of their emotional life. At that time, the aggressive and suicidal side effects on some people were not known. Then again, supposing a post-forget drug was produced, would it necessarily prevent PTSD symptoms? The effect might be like that of rape victims who had been given Rohypnol, who have vague memories of distress and abuse but can't piece together the details of the events, making it difficult to process what happened. This could possibly make Post Traumatic Stress symptoms more distressing and perhaps more opaque, complicating psychological therapy. But wait a moment; I'm spoiling my own story. We have a new drug promising to remove memories of a recent trauma. Let's suppose it was effective and that it left positive memories unscathed. Hypothetically speaking, wouldn't this be a good idea?

After a marketing campaign that raised expectations, and deliberations by NICE and UK government departments, it would probably be treated something like Viagra was in the UK, only to be prescribed by the doctor if specific clinical criteria were met, and then only in limited doses. General Practitioners would likewise have to ensure that the trauma fulfilled certain criteria for seriousness and no co-existing psychiatric disorders were present. The patient would have to be prescribed a limited course of "forget" pills. The trouble is, despite all the government's best planning, Viagra was soon out on the streets and later readily available via the Internet. What was originally presented as a cure for a clinical problem has ended up in the growing larder of recreational drugs. Our "forget" drugs originally administered carefully only to those in real danger of developing PTSD might end up as available to anyone who decided they have a "trauma" – teenagers whose love affair breaks down, stress at work, hurtful comments by others, as well as more serious life-threatening traumas. Each of us would become masters of our own fate, deciding which life events should enter the slate of our memory and which should be eradicated. We would write our own life script.

Experts at the Centre for Cognitive Liberty and Ethics say that memory-erasing drugs are on the way and question whether the legal system is prepared to deal with the change such drugs would bring.[9] They pose questions such as: would individuals have the right to erase their own memories? Would the drugs be prohibited? Would employers be able to make willingness to take a memory-erasing drug a condition for employment? Would it invalidate legal cases? Others, too, question the morality of memory removal "when a fully realised memory removal drug could be used quite maliciously to impose memory loss on individuals who do not chose to use the drug. In fact, I would imagine this would be of interest to countries and terror groups engaged in torture – simply torture someone and then make them forget it ever happened."

Dr Stephen Hyman, a neurobiologist at Harvard,[10] points out that such a drug could be used to erase memories of bad behaviour, even of crimes, pointing out that such "troubling memories – and a healthy dread of them – form the foundation of a moral conscience". Interestingly, one of the scientists developing memory-erasing substances, Joe Tsien of the Medical College of Georgia, Augusta,[11] makes a very basic point. "All memories, even very painful emotional memories, have their purposes. We learn from these experiences to avoid making the same kinds of mistake." One could not really apply this to life-threatening traumas, which are hardly learning experiences in this sense, but it would apply to the stresses and strains of everyday life.

The Natural Solution

In this final chapter I have presented two new movements in trauma research. Post Traumatic Growth carries the message that although trauma is undesirable, and you would not wish anyone to have to go through it, nevertheless positive personal growth can emerge out of the painful struggle to deal with the trauma. It represents growth through adversity. "Memory Erasure" is not anything a person actively does to come to terms with trauma, but by the use of a drug they can block the storage or recall of the memory. Although this does not remove the trauma, it gets as close to removing trauma as possible. One approach represents an acceptance and adaptation, the other rejection and removal.

Emotional Processing provides an alternative solution, which in a way contains the best elements of both approaches. Emotional Processing Therapy has the potential to be incredibly effective with Post Traumatic Stress; it is not unusual for nearly all the symptoms of PTSD to subside to very low levels or to completely fade away. As in grieving for a loved one, their memory is never forgotten – happy and unhappy memories from the past can be recalled – yet without the intense emotional pain of those early days of grief. Likewise, the events of the trauma remain, but their emotional power can be diminished and eradicated through Emotional Processing Therapy. This is superior to a memory-erasing drug, because it deals with the troublesome emotion, leaving the memory intact, rather than eradicating both memory and emotion together. But Emotional Processing Therapy does involve a great struggle and a journey from rejecting emotional memories to accepting and assimilating them. In this way it resembles Post Traumatic Growth. It requires courage to bring out, face, and feel the trauma. Recovery is possible, and often a full recovery. It is a struggle, but in that very struggle are contained the seeds of personal empowerment and achievement.

References

Chapter 1

1 Kessler, R. C., Berglund, P., Demler, O., Jin, R. & Walkers, E. E. (2005). "Lifetime prevalence and age-of-onset distributions of DSM-IV disorders in the National Comorbidity Survey Replication". *Archives of General Psychiatry*, 62, 593–602.

2 Norris, F. H. & Stone, L. B. (2007). "The epidemiology of trauma and PTSD". Chapter 5 in *Handbook of PTSD: Science and Practice*. Eds. M. J. Friedman, T. M. Keane & P. A. Resick. New York: Guilford Press.

3 Breslau, N., Kessler, R. C., Chilcoat, H.D., Schultz, L. R., Davis, G. C. & Andreski, P. (1998). "Trauma and post traumatic stress disorder in the community: the 1996 Detroit area survey of trauma". *Archives of General Psychiatry*, 55, 626–631.

4 Baker, R. (1995). *Understanding Panic Attacks and Overcoming Fear*. Oxford: Lion Hudson.

Chapter 2

1 American Psychiatric Association (1994). *Diagnostic and Statistical Manual of Mental Disorders*, 4th edition. Washington DC: American Psychiatric Association.

2 Janis, I. L. (1951). *Air War and Emotional Stress: Psychological studies of bombing and civilian defense*. Westport, Connecticut: Greenwood Press.

3 Crocq, M. A., Macher, J. P., Barros-Beck, J. et al. (1993). "Post traumatic stress disorder in World War II prisoners of war from Alsace-Lorraine who survived captivity in the USSR". *International Handbook of Traumatic Stress Syndromes*. Eds. J. P. Wilson & B. Raphael. New York: Plenum Press.

4 Resick, P. A. & Schnicke, M. K. (1993). *Cognitive Processing Therapy for Rape Victims*. Newbury Park: Sage Publications.

5 Lifton, R. J. (1967). *Death in Life: Survivors of Hiroshima*. New York: Random House.

6 Shatan, C. F. (1978). "Stress disorder among Vietnam veterans: the emotional content of combat continues". *Stress Disorders Among Vietnam Veterans*. Ed. C. R. Figley. New York: Brunner/Mazel.

7 "Sense of foreshortened future". www.ptsdforum.org. Accessed 23 July 2009.

8 Resick, P. A. & Schnicke, M. K. (1993). *Cognitive Processing Therapy for Rape Victims*. Newbury Park: Sage Publications.

9 Raphael, B. (1986). *When Disaster Strikes*. London: Hutchinson.

Chapter 3

1 American Psychiatric Association (1994). *Diagnostic and Statistical Manual of Mental Disorders*, 4th edition. Washington DC: American Psychiatric Association.

2 Friedman, M. J., Resick, P. A. & Keane, T. M. (2007). "PTSD: twenty-five years of progress and challenges". *Handbook of PTSD: Science and Practice*. Eds. M. J. Friedman, T. M. Keane & P. A. Resick. New York: Guildford Press.

Chapter 5

1 Baker, R. (2007). *Emotional Processing: Healing Through Feeling*. Oxford: Lion Hudson.

2 Rachman, S. (1980). "Emotional processing". *Behaviour Research and Therapy*, 18, 51–60.

3 Baker, R., Holloway, J., Thomas, P. W., Thomas, S., Owens, M. (2004). "Emotional processing and panic". *Behaviour Research and Therapy*, 42, 1271–1287.

4 Baker, R., Thomas, S., Thomas, P. W. & Owens, M. (2007). "Development of an Emotional Processing Scale". *Journal of Psychosomatic Research*, 62, 167–178.

5 Brosschot, J. F. & Aarsse, H. R. (2001). "Restrictive emotional processing and somatic attribution in fibromyalgia". *International Journal of Psychiatry in Medicine*, 31, 27–146.

6 Rachman, S. (2001). "Emotional processing, with special reference to post traumatic stress disorder". *International Review of Psychiatry*, 13, 164–171.

7 Foa, E. B. & Kozak, M. J. (1986). "Emotional processing of fear: exposure to corrective information". *Psychological Bulletin*, 99, 20–35.

8 oa, E. B., Huppert, J. D. & Cahill, S. P. (2006). "Emotional Processing Theory: an update". *Pathological Anxiety: Emotional*

processing in etiology and treatment, Part 1. Ed. B. O. Rothbaum. New York: Guilford Press.

9 McFarlane, A. C., Girolamo, G. D. (1996). "The nature of traumatic stressors and the epidemiology of post traumatic reactions". Chapter 7 in *Traumatic Stress*. Eds. B. A. van der Kolk, A. C. McFarlane & L. Weisaeth. New York: Guilford Press.

10 Ursano, R. J., McCaughey, B. G. & Fullerton, C. S. (1994). *Individual and Community Responses to Trauma and Disaster*. Cambridge: Cambridge University Press.

11 Raphael, B. (1986). *When Disaster Strikes*. London: Hutchinson.

Chapter 6

1 Brewin, C. R., Watson, M., McCarthy, S. et al. (1998). "Intrusive memories and depression in cancer patients". *Behaviour Research and Therapy*, 36, 1131–1142.

2 Brewin, C. R. (2007). "Remembering and forgetting". Chapter 7 in *Handbook of PTSD: Science and Practice*. Eds. M. J. Friedman, T. M. Keane & P. A. Resick. New York: Guilford Press.

3 Grey, N., Homes, E. & Brewin, C. R. (2001). "Peritraumatic emotional 'hot spots' in memory". *Behavioural and Cognitive Psychotherapy*, 29, 357–362.

4 Epstein, S. (1988). "Emotions and psychopathology from the perspective of cognitive-experiential self-theory". *Emotions in Psychopathology*. Eds. W. F. Flack and J. D. Laird. New York: Oxford University Press.

5 Bucci, W. (1997). *Psychoanalysis and Cognitive Science: A multiple code theory*. New York: Guilford Press.

6 Bucci, W. (2001). "Pathways of emotional communication". *Psychoanalytic Enquiry* 21, 40.

7 "What is Emotional Processing?". www.emotionalprocessing.org. uk. Accessed 31 July 2009.

8 Leventhal, H. (1979). "A perceptual motor processing model of emotion". In *Perception of Emotion in Self and Others Vol 5*. Eds. P. Pliner, K. R. Blankstein & I. M. Spigel. New York: Plenum Press.

9 Teasdale, J. D. (1999). "Emotional processing, three modes of mind and the prevention of relapse in depression". *Behaviour Research and Therapy*, 37, 937–977.

10 Brewin, C. R., Dalgleish, T. & Joseph, S. (1996). "A dual representation theory of post traumatic stress disorder". *Psychological Review*, 103, 670–686.

11 De Prince, A. P. & Freyd, J. J. (2007). "Trauma-induced dissociation". Chapter 8 in *Handbook of PTSD: Science and Practice*. Eds. M. J. Friedman, T. M. Keane & P. A. Resick. New York: Guilford Press.

12 Van der Kolk, B. A., van der Hart, O. & Marmar, C. R. (1996). "Dissociation and information processing in post traumatic stress disorder". Chapter 13 in *Traumatic Stress*. Eds. B. A. van der Kolk, A. C. McFarlane & L. Weiseath. New York: Guilford Press.

13 Baker, R. (2007). *Emotional Processing: Healing Through Feeling*. Oxford: Lion Hudson.

14 Baker, R., Thomas, S., Thomas, P. W. & Owens, M. (2007). "Development of an Emotional Processing Scale". *Journal of Psychosomatic Research*, 62, 167–178.

15 Gross, J. J. & Thompson, R. A. P. (2007). "Emotion regulation: conceptual foundations". *Handbook of Emotion Regulation*. Ed. J. J. Gross. New York: Guilford Press.

16 Richards, J. M. & Gross, J. J. (2000). "Emotion regulation and memory: the cognition costs of keeping one's cool". *Journal of Personality and Social Psychology*, 79, 410–424.

17 Salters-Pedneault, K., Tull, M. T., Roemer, L. (2004). "The role of avoidance of emotional material in anxiety disorders". *Applied and Preventative Psychology*, 11, 95–114.

18 Baker, R. (2003). *Understanding Panic Attacks and Overcoming Fear*. Oxford: Lion Hudson.

Chapter 7

1 Baker, R. (2007). *Emotional Processing: Healing Through Feeling*. Oxford: Lion Hudson.

2 Bucci, W. (2001). "Pathways of emotional communication", *Psychoanalytic Enquiry*, 21, 40.

3 Gendlin, E. T. (1981). *Focusing*, 2nd edition. New York: Bantam Books.

4 Rogers, C. R. (1961). *On Becoming a Person: A Therapist's View of Psychotherapy*. London: Constable.

5 Paivio, S. C. & Greenberg, L. S. (1998). "Experiential theory of emotion". *Emotions in Psychopathology*. Eds. W. F. Flack & J. D. Laird. New York: Oxford University Press.

6 Rogers, C. R. (1961). "To be that self which one truly is". *On Becoming a Person: A Therapist's View of Psychotherapy*. London: Constable.

7 Ortony, A., Collins, A. & Clore, G. L. (1988). *The Cognitive Structure of Emotions*. Cambridge: Cambridge University Press.

8 Oatley, K. & Duncan, E. (1994). "The experience of emotions in everyday life". *Cognition in Emotion*, 8, 369–381.

9 Mogg, K. & Bradley, B. P. (1998). "A cognitive-motivational analysis of anxiety". *Behaviour Research and Therapy*, 36, 809–848.

10 Beck, A. T. (1976). *Cognitive Therapy and the Emotional Disorders*. New York: International University Press.

11 Baker, R. (2003). *Understanding Panic Attacks and Overcoming Fear*. Oxford: Lion Hudson.

12 Young, J. E. & Klosko, J. S. (1994). *Reinventing Your Life: How to break free from negative life patterns*. New York: Penguin Group.

13 Foa, E. B., Hembree, E. A., Rothbaum, B. O. (2007). *Prolonged Exposure Therapy for PTSD*. Oxford: Oxford University Press.

14 Brewin, C. R. & Holmes, E. A. (2003). "Psychological theories of post traumatic stress disorder". *Clinical Psychology Review*, 23, 339–376.

15 Mesquita, B. (2001). "Culture and emotions: different approaches to the question". Chapter 7 in *Emotions: Current Issues and Future Directions*. Eds. T. J. Mayne & G. A. Bonanno. New York: Guilford Press.

16 Caspi, A., Elder, G. H. & Bem. D. J. (1987). "Moving against the world: life-course patterns of explosive children". *Developmental Psychology*, 23, 308–313.

17 Olweus, D. (1979). "Stability of aggressive reaction patterns in males: a review". *Psychological Bulletin*, 86, 852–875.

18 Rubin, K. H. (1993). "The Waterloo longitudinal project: correlates and consequences of social withdrawal in childhood". *Social Withdrawal, Inhibition and Shyness in Childhood*. Eds. K. H. Rubin & J. Asendorpf. Hillsdale, NJ: Erlbaum.

19 Jenkins, J. M., & Oatley, K. (1998). "Emotion schemas in children". Chapter 3 of *Emotions in Psychopathology*. Eds. W. F. Flack & J. D. Laird. New York: Oxford University Press.

20 Gendlin, E. T. (1996). *Focusing-Oriented Psychotherapy: A manual of the experiential method*. New York: Guilford Press.

21 Greenberg, L. S., Rice, L. N. & Elliott, R. (1993). *Facilitating Emotional Change: The moment-by-moment process*. New York: Guilford Press.

22 Kennedy-Moore, E. & Watson, J. C. (1999). *Expressing Emotion*. New York: Guilford Press.

23 Scheff, T. J. (1979) *Catharsis in Healing, Ritual, and Drama.* Berkeley: University of California Press.

24 Bohart, A. C. (1980). "Towards a cognitive theory of catharsis". *Psychotherapy: Theory, research and practice*, 17, 192–201.

25 Pennebaker, J. W. (1997). *Opening Up: The healing power of expressing emotions.* New York: Guilford Press.

26 Gross, J. J. & Thompson, R. A. P. (2007). "Emotion regulation: conceptual foundations". *Handbook of Emotion Regulation.* Ed. J. J. Gross. New York: Guilford Press.

Chapter 9

1 Tichener, J. L. & Ross, W. D. (1974). "Acute or chronic stress as determinants of behaviour, character and neurosis". In *American Handbook of Psychiatry.* Eds. S. Arieti & E. C. Brody. New York: Basic Books.

2 McFarlane, A. C. & Papay, P. (1992). "Multiple diagnoses in post traumatic stress disorder in the victims of a natural disaster". *Journal of Nervous and Mental Disease*, 180 (8), 498–504.

3 Goldberg, J., True, W. R., Eisen, S. A. et al. (1990). "A twin study of the effects of the Vietnam war on post traumatic stress disorder". *Journal of the American Medical Association*, 263(9), 1227–1232.

4 Shalev, A. Y. (1992). "Post traumatic stress disorder among injured survivors of a terrorist attack". *Journal of Nervous and Mental Disease*, 180, 505–509.

5 Solomon, Z. (1993). *Combat stress reaction: the enduring toll of war.* New York: Plenum Press.

6 Mayou, R., Bryant, B. & Duthie, R. (1993). "Psychiatric consequences of road traffic accidents". *British Medical Journal*, 307, 647–651.

7 Malt, U., Karlehagen, S., Hoff, H. et al. (1993). "The effect of major railway accidents on the psychological health of train drivers". *Journal of Psychosomatic Research*, 37 (8), 793–805.

8 Solomon, Z. (1993). *Combat stress reaction: the enduring toll of war.* New York: Plenum Press.

9 Solomon, Z., Laror, N. & McFarlane, A. C. (1996). "Acute post traumatic reactions in soldiers and civilians". Chapter 5 in *Traumatic Stress.* Eds. B. A. van der Kolk, A. C. McFarlane & L. Weisaeth. New York: Guilford Press.

10 Shalev, A. Y., Schreiber, S. & Galai, T. (1993). "Early psychiatric

responses to traumatic injury". *Journal of Traumatic Stress*, 6, 441–450.

11 Shalev, A. Y., Peri, T., Canetti, L. & Schreiber, S. (1996). "Predictors of PTSD in injured trauma survivors". *American Journal of Psychiatry*, 53, 224–291.

12 Wessely, S., Bisson, J. & Rose, S. (2000). "A systematic review of brief psychological interventions ('debriefing') for the treatment of immediate trauma related symptoms and the prevention of post traumatic stress disorder". *Depression, Anxiety and Neurosis module of the Cochrane Database of Systematic Reviews*. Eds. M. Oakley Browne, R. Churchill, D. Gill et al. Oxford Update Software.

13 Wessely, S. & Deahl, M. (2003). "Psychological debriefing is a waste of time". *British Journal of Psychiatry*, 183, 12–14.

14 Wegner, D. M. (1998). "Ironic processes of mental control". *Psychological Review*, 101, 34–52.

15 Wegner, D. M., Schneider, D. J., Carter, S. R. & White, T. L. (1987). "Paradoxical effects of thought suppression". *Journal of Personality and Social Psychology*, 53, 5–13.

16 Lutz, T. (1999). *Crying: The natural and cultural history of tears*. New York: Norton.

Chapter 10

1 Foa, E. B. & Kozak, M. J. (1986). "Emotional processing of fear: exposure to corrective information". *Psychological Bulletin*, 99, 20–35.

2 Gendlin, E. T. (1996). *Focusing-Oriented Psychotherapy: A manual of the experiential method*. New York: Guilford Press.

3 Rogers, C. R. (1961). *On Becoming a Person: A Therapist's View of Psychotherapy*. London: Constable.

4 Greenberg, L. S., Rice, L. N. & Elliott, R. (1993). *Facilitating Emotional Change: The moment-by-moment process*. New York: Guilford Press.

5 Freud, S. (1909). "Selected papers on hysteria and other psychoneuroses". No. 4 of the *Neurosis and Mental Disease* Monograph Series. New York.

6 Kennedy-Moore, E. & Watson, J. C. (1999). *Expressing Emotion*. New York: Guilford Press.

7 Pennebaker, J. W. (1997). *Opening Up: The healing power of expressing emotions*. New York: Guilford Press.

8 Whelton, W. J. (2004). "Emotional processes in psychotherapy:

evidence across therapeutic modalities". *Clinical Psychology and Psychotherapy*, 11, 58–71.

9 Nicols, M. P., & Zax, M. (1977). *Catharsis in Psychotherapy*. New York: Gardner.

10 Freud, S. (1910). "The origin of psychoanalysis". Reprinted in *A General Selection from the Works of Freud*. Ed. J. Rickman. London: Hogarth Press.

11 National Institute for Health and Clinical Excellence (2005). "Post Traumatic Stress Disorder. Clinical Guidelines CG26". www.nice.org.uk/CG26. Accessed 31 July 2009.

12 Foa, E. B., Hembree, E. A., Rothbaum, B. O. (2007). *Prolonged Exposure Therapy for PTSD*. Oxford: Oxford University Press.

13 Foa, E. B. & Rothbaum, B. O. (1998). *Treating the Trauma of Rape*. New York: Guilford Press.

14 Foa, E. B. & Kozak, M. J. (1986). "Emotional processing of fear: exposure to corrective information". *Psychological Bulletin*, 99, 20–35.

15 Grey, N., Young, K. & Holmes, E. (2002). "Cognitive restructuring within reliving: a treatment for peritraumatic emotional 'hot spots' in post traumatic stress disorder". *Behavioural and Cognitive Psychotherapy*, 30, 37–56.

16 Marks, I. M. (1978). "Exposure treatments: clinical applications". *Behaviour Modification: Principles and Clinical Applications,* 2nd edition. Ed. W. S. Agras. Boston: Little, Brown & Co.

17 Ramsay, R. W. (1977). "Behavioural approaches to bereavement". *Behaviour Research and Therapy*, 5, 131–135.

18 Blakey, R. & Baker, R. (1980). "An exposure approach to alcohol abuse". *Behaviour Research and Therapy*, 18, 319–325.

19 Frijda, N. H. (2007). *The Laws of Emotion*. New York: Routledge.

20 Baker, R. (2003). *Understanding Panic Attacks and Overcoming Fear*. Oxford: Lion Hudson.

21 McFadyen, M. (1989). "The cognitive invalidation approach to panic". Chapter 13 in *Panic Disorder: Theory, research and therapy*. Ed. R. Baker. Chichester: John Wiley.

22 Kelly, G. A. (1963). *A Theory of Personality*. New York: Norton.

23 Baker, R. & McFadyen, M. (1986). "Cognitive invalidation and the enigma of exposure". *Current Issues in Clinical Psychology Vol. 2*. Ed. E. Karas. New York: Plenum Press.

24 Brewin, C. R. (2007). "Remembering and forgetting". Chapter 7 in *Handbook of PTSD: Science and Practice*. Eds. M. J. Friedman, T. M.

Keane & P. A. Resick. New York: Guilford Press.

25 Bucci, W. (2001). "Pathways of emotional communication". *Psychoanalytic Enquiry* 21, 40.

26 Scheff, T. J. (1979). *Catharsis in Healing, Ritual, and Drama*. Berkeley: University of California Press.

27 Bohart, A. C. (1980). "Towards a cognitive theory of catharsis". *Psychotherapy: Theory, research and practice*, 17, 192–201.

28 Freud, S. (1909). "Selected papers on hysteria and other psychoneuroses". No. 4 of the *Neurosis and Mental Disease* Monograph Series. New York.

29 Whelton, W. J. (2004). "Emotional processes in psychotherapy: evidence across therapeutic modalities". *Clinical Psychology and Psychotherapy*, 11, 58–71.

30 Rogers, C. R. (1951). *Client-Centred Therapy*. New York: Mifflin.

Chapter 11

1 Davidson, J. R. T. (1996). "Davidson Trauma Scale". New York: Multi Health Systems Inc.

2 Bedford, A. & Foulds, G. A. (1978). *Manual of the Delusions-Symptoms-States Inventory*. Windsor: NFER-Nelson.

3. Rosenberg, M. (1965). "Society and the adolescent self-image". Princeton, NJ: Princeton University Press.

Chapter 12

1 National Institute for Health and Clinical Excellence (2005). "Post Traumatic Stress Disorder. Clinical Guidelines CG26". www.nice.org.uk/CG26. Accessed 31 July 2009.

2 Resick, P. A., Monson, C. M., Gutner, C. (2007). "Psychosocial treatment of PTSD". Chapter 17 in *Handbook of PTSD: Science and Practice*. Eds. M. J. Friedman, T. M. Keane & P. A. Resick. New York: Guilford Press.

3 Brewin, C. R. & Holmes, E. A. (2003). "Psychological theories of post traumatic stress disorder". *Clinical Psychology Review*, 23, 339–376.

4 Foa, E. B., Hembree, E. A., Rothbaum, B. O. (2007). *Prolonged Exposure Therapy for PTSD*. Oxford: Oxford University Press.

5 Foa, E. B., Huppert, J. D. & Cahill, S. P. (2006). "Emotional Processing Theory: an update". *Pathological Anxiety: Emotional processing in etiology and treatment, Part 1*. Ed. B. O. Rothbaum. New York: Guilford Press.

Chapter 13

1 Baker, R. (2007). *Emotional Processing: Healing Through Feeling*. Oxford: Lion Hudson.

2 Baker, R., Holloway, J., Thomas, P. W., Thomas, S., Owens, M. (2004). "Emotional processing and panic". *Behaviour Research and Therapy*, 42, 1271–1287.

3 Baker, R., Thomas, S., Thomas, P. W. & Owens, M. (2007). "Development of an Emotional Processing Scale". *Journal of Psychosomatic Research*, 62, 167–178.

4 Emotional Processing website. www.emotionalprocessing.org.uk. Accessed 31 July 2009.

5 Wilkins, C., Baker, R., Bick, D. & Thomas, P. (2009). "Emotional processing in childbirth: a predictor of postnatal depression?". *British Journal of Midwifery*, 17(3), 154–159.

6 Raleigh, J. (2004). "A preliminary comparative study of emotional processing in women with fibromyalgia syndrome, rheumatoid arthritis and healthy subjects". M. Sc. thesis, Southampton University.

7 Lothian, S. (2002). "Emotional processing deficits in colorectal cancer: a theoretical overview and empirical investigation". Ph. D. thesis, Southampton University.

8 Baker, R., Thomas, S., Thomas, P. W. & Owens, M. (2007). "Development of an Emotional Processing Scale". *Journal of Psychosomatic Research*, 62, 167–178.

Chapter 15

1 Van der Kolk, B. A. (2007). "The history of trauma in psychiatry". *Handbook of PTSD: Science and Practice*. Eds. M. J. Friedman, T. M. Keane & P. A. Resick. New York: Guilford Press.

Chapter 16

1 Kelly, G. A. (1963). *A Theory of Personality*. New York: Norton.

Chapter 17

1 *7/7: The Miracle of Carriage 346*. TV documentary screened on More 4 on 4 July 2009.

2 *7/7: The Angels of Edgeware Road*. TV documentary screened on More 4 on 4 July 2009.

3 Tedeschi, R. G. & Calhoun, L. G. (2004). "Post traumatic growth: a new perspective on psychotraumatology". *Psychiatric Times*, 21(4).

4 Tedeschi, R. G., Park, C. L. & Calhoun, L. G. (Eds.) (1998). *Post traumatic growth: Positive changes in the aftermath of crisis*. New Jersey: Lawrence Erlbaum Associates.

5 Turner, de Sales, Cox, H. (2004). "Facilitating post traumatic growth". *Health and Quality of Life Outcomes*, 2, 34.

6 Young, William P. (2008). *The Shack*. London: Hodder & Stoughton.

7 Tedeschi, R. G. & Calhoun, L. G. (2004). "Post traumatic growth: a new perspective on psychotraumatology". *Psychiatric Times*, 21(4).

8 Carey, B. (2009). "Brain researchers open door to editing memory". *The New York Times*. 6 April 2009.

9 Centre for Cognitive Liberty and Ethics (2009). Accessed at www.cognitiveliberty.org/news/paycheck.html on 31 July 2009.

10 Ibid.

11 Callaway, E. (2008). "'Eternal Sunshine' drug selectively erases memories". www.newscientist.com/article/dn15025-eternal-sunshine-drug-selectively-erases-memories.html. Accessed 31 July 2009.

Index